trotman

# Psychology
## UNCOVERED

Owen Davies

*Psychology Uncovered*

This first edition published by Trotman, an imprint of Crimson Publishing Limited, Westminster House, Kew Road, Richmond, Surrey, TW9 2ND.

© Trotman Publishing 2009

**Author:** Owen Davies

**British Library Cataloguing in Publication Data**
A catalogue record for this book is available from the British Library

ISBN: 978 1 84455 202 3

Typeset by RefineCatch Ltd, Bungay, Suffolk

Printed and bound in Italy by Lego SpA

# CONTENTS

Introduction                                                    v

1.  What is Psychology?                                          1

2.  Choosing a Specialism                                       13

3.  Clinical Psychology                                         36

4.  Educational Psychology                                      52

5.  Neuropsychology                                             68

6.  Forensic Psychology                                         82

7.  Occupational Psychology                                     96

8.  Health, Sport and Exercise Psychology                      110

9.  Training, Skills and Qualifications                        127

10. Finding Your First Job                                     141

11. Career Progression                                         155

12. Finding out More                                           162

# INTRODUCTION

This book describes the many career options open to people who have studied psychology. This means it will cover a wide range of careers, many of which will not have the word 'psychologist' in the job title.

There is a detailed description of six of the most important areas – clinical psychology, neuropsychology, educational psychology, forensic psychology, occupational psychology, and health, sport and exercise psychology. There are also rather shorter descriptions of the very many other types of work for which psychology training and qualifications are useful. These may relate to health and social care, community work, education, and work within organisations (for example as an equality, training or human resources officer).

The aims are to:

■ describe what work you would do if you chose a particular career option

■ explain what qualifications and training you would need

■ show where you can find more detailed information about each of the options that you might consider

■ help you to think about which career might be most suitable.

# THE STRUCTURE

The chapters in this book are grouped into three parts.

- Chapter 1 explains what psychology is, and how an understanding of it is used in the fields of health, social care, community work, education, and in public and private organisations. Chapter 2 gives specific information about 50 careers that use the skills, knowledge and understanding that are gained by studying psychology.

- Chapters 3 to 8 then describe six particularly important fields: clinical and educational psychology, neuropsychology, forensic, occupational, health and sport psychology. By looking at the chapter or chapters that relate most closely to your interests you will be able to find out more about your possible career options. The focus of each chapter is on the role of chartered psychologists (for example, a clinical psychologist who works in a hospital mental health team) but it will also be of interest to those thinking of related roles (such as counsellor or mental health worker).

- The last three chapters then look at how you can more carefully assess your own suitability for a particular career. Chapter 9 looks at the training and qualifications that you will need, and the skills and attributes that are required. Chapter 10 gives guidance on how you can go about finding your first job. Chapter 11 encourages you to think about the long term: as well as thinking about the next five years it's important to try to think forward and imagine what it will be like working in a particular career in 10, 20 and perhaps even 40 years' time.

# REFERENCES AND LINKS

Throughout every chapter you will find references to websites and organisations where you can find more detailed information. These have also been collected together in Chapter 12 so that you can easily refer to the ones that you think are most relevant.

Note that the references to websites generally take you to the homepage. You will then need to search that site for specific information on, for example, career prospects, the qualifications needed or examples of recruitment advertisements. This approach has been taken to avoid problems when the structure and content of the website is changed.

# TERMINOLOGY

The terminology used in different fields of psychology can become quite confusing. For example, a counselling psychologist will typically refer to carrying out therapy with a 'client', while a psychiatrist or the client's GP surgery will refer to the person as a 'patient'. Health managers and politicians may refer to 'customers', and that term will certainly be used by psychologists working for marketing departments in private companies. And community workers and social workers may refer to 'service users'.

To avoid confusion, a single term, 'client', is used throughout this book.

# USING THIS BOOK IN PRACTICE

This book is designed to be used in many ways by different readers. You may well find that you study some chapters in some detail, dip into others and perhaps ignore some altogether.

For example, if you start with little knowledge of psychology careers, it will probably be most useful to read Chapters 1 and 2, and then select the most relevant one from Chapters 3 to 8. This may be sufficient to show you what areas of psychology are most relevant to you and may suggest future courses of study.

On the other hand, if you are already studying for a psychology degree you may well be able to skim-read Chapter 1, and use Chapter 2 as a way of making preliminary choices about career options. You can then focus on one of Chapters 3 to 8 and also look in detail at Chapters 9 to 11.

However, since different readers will use the text in very different ways, there is inevitably some repetition. For example, Chapter 3 to 8 all contain references to the process of working towards chartered status with the British Psychological Society, and this process is also described in more detail in Chapter 9.

# THE KEY FACTORS TO THINK ABOUT

As you work through the following chapters you will find a great deal of information about careers in psychology. As with studying all reference books, you may begin to feel as though you are being engulfed by information. To minimise this risk the information is presented in a systematic way so that Chapters 3 to 8 focus in turn on six key questions relating to each career.

1 **What do these psychologists do?** This begins with a description of a typical case load, showing some of the typical tasks that you might be doing each day. It then describes the work in more detail, giving information about how the psychologist will use their theoretical understanding to make a practical difference to people and their lives.

2 **Where do they work?** If you followed this career, would you be working in a hospital, health centre, office or sports centre? Or might you be travelling around meeting clients in their workplace or home?

3 **What qualifications are required?** Many careers in psychology require further study, for example, for a doctorate, master's or diploma. This study often requires work experience, training in exactly those work situations that you will meet throughout your career. Certain careers also require you to gain accreditation with a professional body such as the British Psychological Society (BPS) or the Chartered Institute of Personnel and Development (CIPD).

4 **How can I study for this career?** You will see what study you might need to complete if you are, for example, a school or college student, a person applying for university study from outside the UK, a mature student applying for a degree or a graduate returning to study after some years in work.

5 **What's the work really like?** The case study describes the career of a psychologist working in a particular field. The case studies in each chapter should give you an idea of the range of reasons why people select their chosen field, and the very different career paths that they follow.

6   **Is this the career for me?** The final section of each chapter starts
    by describing some practical factors, such as typical salaries and
    working conditions. You can then complete the self-assessment,
    thinking in turn about the tasks involved, the skills and attributes
    that you will need, and the high points and low points. As you work
    through these, they should enable you to think about the most
    important question: 'Can I see myself doing this work throughout my
    career?'

# Chapter One
# WHAT IS PSYCHOLOGY?

Psychology is a science, the study of how people perceive, think, feel and act. Some psychologists carry out research, trying to find out more and adding to our understanding of behaviour. Others use their knowledge and understanding to help individuals, especially those who are suffering psychological stress of some kind, those who find it difficult to function effectively, or those who have mental health problems or some form of disability. A third group use their understanding of psychology within organisations, for example working with managers to develop suitable training, ensure equality and diversity, or help people with their career development.

As you study the various careers in psychology you'll find that all of them involve one or more of the three elements: studying people, using the knowledge when working with individuals and using the knowledge within organisations.

## STUDYING AND USING PSYCHOLOGY

The examples in the following box show some of the typical questions that psychologists may study. In every case you'll see that the knowledge gained can be used later in practical situations.

## Psychology: some typical questions

What effect does watching television have on children and their behaviour?

How do you train a person with learning difficulties to go shopping?

How might a person react after a major accident or being abused in their childhood?

How should teachers or parents deal with a child's tantrums?

What is the best way of planning shifts so that people can work effectively at three o'clock in the morning?

What is the most effective way to prevent criminals re-offending?

In all the examples, you will probably be able to think of a common-sense answer. For example, some people will have a common-sense view that criminals can only be prevented from re-offending by locking them up in prison. To others it seems to be common sense that education and therapy will be more effective, and that prison is actually more likely to lead to further offences.

Only research can show which of the approaches is more effective. But once the research has been done, it can be used in relation to each of the other two aspects of psychologists' work described above. The knowledge can be used when working with individual offenders, for example, when deciding what sort of institution a prisoner should go to, or what therapy they might need. That knowledge can also be used when working with the whole organisation to decide what training prison officers may need, what shifts will work best, and so on.

## Psychology and other disciplines

Psychology relates to many other different disciplines, including biology, medicine, linguistics, philosophy, anthropology, sociology and artificial intelligence.

As an example, think of the adult who has difficulty speaking. It may be that the problem is linked to a biological problem, such as damage caused by an accident, or is a medical problem that can be alleviated using drugs. It may need speech therapy based on an understanding of linguistics. The difficulties the person will have in society can be understood by looking at the findings of sociological and anthropological research. Of course, some may think that society should not spend limited funds on this person, a point of view that needs to be considered from the various philosophical viewpoints.

Looking at the various psychology courses at university, you'll see that many of them combine psychology with other disciplines. For example, at the time of writing Bristol University offers undergraduate courses in psychology, psychology and philosophy, and psychology and zoology.

## Branches of the study of psychology

Within psychology, there are many branches, each of which may provide insight into particular aspects of how people perceive, think, feel and act. Some of the most important are summarised below.

**Clinical psychology** relates to the study, analysis, prevention and relief of psychologically based problems such as addictions, depression, personality disorders or post-traumatic stress. The main areas of study relate to assessment of the individual, selecting a suitable approach to treatment, and the various types of therapy. Clinical psychology should not be confused with psychiatry, which is a field studied by medically qualified practitioners who typically tend to focus on drug-based solutions.

**Cognitive psychology** is an area of study relating to internal mental processes such as problem-solving, memory and language. It looks at how we understand, diagnose and solve problems. What are the mental processes by which we respond to stimuli; what mental rules do we follow when deciding how close we can get to a fire?

**Developmental psychology** looks at the ways in which people change over their lifetime. The main areas of focus are on child development, adolescence and old age. When considering young children, for example, there is the question about the extent to which development is based on 'nature' (the genetic elements of behaviour that are inherited from the parents) and 'nurture' (the elements that result from the influences of the parents, the family and wider society). How important are early relations with the mother? To what extent do children learn in a systematic way, building on their earlier understanding?

**Evolutionary psychologists** consider that the development of mental and psychological traits has occurred in a way that corresponds to the evolutionary development of species. For example, they suggest that all peoples have developed an ability to speak, and hypothesise that this is an inherited trait; in contrast, not all peoples have developed writing, and so evolutionary psychologists assume that writing and reading are solely learned behaviours.

**Forensic psychology** relates to the use of psychology in the criminal justice system. It commonly involves assessing whether the accused is mentally competent to stand trial. Forensic psychologists also provide sentencing recommendations, treatment recommendations, information about mitigating factors, assessment of future risk and evaluation of the creditability of witnesses.

**Health psychology** is the study of how biology, people's behaviour and the social environment may influence health and illness. So, for example, a health psychologist may try to identify the likely effects of many inter-related factors such as individuals' lifestyles, their parents' health, dietary habits, and the influence of environmental factors such as traffic pollution.

**Neuropsychology** is the study of the structure and function of the brain, and of how this may affect psychological processes and overt behaviours. For example, it may involve studying scans of the brain to investigate which areas are involved in particular activities, or using standardised tests to analyse a person's particular strengths and weaknesses.

**Social psychology** looks at how people and groups interact. Social psychologists investigate how the thoughts, feelings and behaviours of individuals are influenced by other people. For example, to what extent does peer pressure act on young people in relation to their studies, social habits, attitudes to violence, and so on?

# WHAT DO PSYCHOLOGISTS DO?

Having looked at the various branches of psychology, you should now be better able to think about the work that different types of psychologist do. The British Psychological Society (www.bps.org.uk) explains that psychologists work in many different areas of society and are concerned with working with people's practical problems. Some of the problem areas in which they work include:

■ helping people to overcome depression, stress, trauma or phobias

■ easing the effects of parental divorce on children

■ speeding up recovery from brain injury

■ helping to stop or prevent bullying at school or in the workplace

■ ensuring that school pupils and students are being taught in the most effective way

■ making sure that people are happy at work and perform to the best of their abilities

■ helping the police, courts and prison service to perform more effectively

■ helping athletes and sports people to perform better.

Of course, that's only a few examples from a very long list of activities that a psychologist may carry out. It's also focused on the work of people who work as chartered psychologists (for example, clinical, counselling, forensic or occupational psychologists).

If you add the very many other jobs that use a psychologist's skills and training, you could also include other examples. University lecturers and government researchers carry out research into psychological issues. Teachers with special skills may teach children and young adults with learning difficulties or mental health problems. Ergonomists investigate the ways in which people use equipment and machines, and plan how they can use them safely and most effectively. Equality and diversity officers work to ensure equality and diversity within organisations, and promote the benefits of those policies. And a consumer psychologist works within commercial and public organisations to study the behaviour and preferences of actual and potential customers.

## The skills required

The skills that a psychologist needs will, of course, vary depending on the type of work. A psychologist working with a distressed child will need very different skills from a psychologist researching the effects of a particular government health programme or a psychologist trying to motivate an athlete recovering from a major injury.

However, it's likely that psychologists will generally need skills in the following broad areas.

- **Listening and observing.** Many aspects of a psychologist's work involve listening to people and perhaps identifying the underlying messages of what they are saying. They also need to be able to observe and interpret the person's body language.

- **Communication.** Psychologists will often also need to communicate their own thoughts and ideas to the client and to other professionals. Finally, they need to be able to produce clear, concise written reports, perhaps explaining rather complex ideas to people with little or no specialist knowledge.

- **Problem-solving.** Many aspects of psychological work involve solving problems. For example, having spent an hour in a meeting with a child, the educational psychologist must decide what actions are most likely to improve his or her learning or social skills. The psychologist who carries out research must have a good understanding of scientific techniques so that other professionals will be convinced of the value of the research findings.

- **Team-worker skills.** Many psychologists work as members of teams, generally working with professionals from other backgrounds. To work effectively in mixed teams of this type, the psychologist is going to need patience and tact, and may have to work to motivate the other members of their team and the various clients. Finally, their overall levels of skills and behaviour must inspire trust and confidence in clients and co-workers.

■ **Research.** Psychologists working in many areas of work need to measure the effectiveness of themselves, their techniques, or the wider organisation. Research methods form an important element in most psychology degrees and are an essential element in most postgraduate programmes.

The topic of skills, attributes and qualifications is discussed in greater detail in Chapter 9.

# WORKING AS A PSYCHOLOGIST

Since the range of careers for psychologists is so wide, it is difficult to be specific about the pay and working conditions of 'psychologists'. You will find more detailed descriptions in the later chapters of this book and in the various websites that are referenced in the text. What follows are some general comments that apply to most psychologist roles.

## Hours

Psychologists typically work about 37 hours a week, Monday to Friday, but part-time work is often available, particularly in the health and social care field. Working hours are mainly nine to five, though some evening or weekend work may be involved in certain roles (for example, in health, social care or community work). For some roles there may be an on-call system to cover emergency situations.

## Working environment

Most psychologists work in large towns and cities, though a few (for example, those working in prisons or residential schools) may work in rural areas.

As a psychologist, your work would usually be based in an office, but you would probably also need to spend time in other locations. For example psychologists in health and social care may have to spend some time in clinics, hospital wards and other health care settings; educational psychologists visit schools and residential special schools; forensic psychologists work in prisons and young offender institutions, and so on.

Many psychologists work part-time for an organisation and also offer their services as freelancers or consultants. For example, a counselling psychologist may work three days a week for the NHS and also work two days as a private consultant working from home or for a private health care provider. An occupational psychologist working in an organisation may decide to gain further qualifications as a sports psychologist and then work part-time with a local sports team.

## Chartered Psychologist Status

Many job roles are only open to psychologists who have, or are working towards, chartered psychologist status. This is explained in detail in Chapter 9, but basically is open to those who have studied a psychology degree accredited by the British Psychological Society, have a further qualification (most commonly a doctorate in an accredited course, such as clinical psychology or health psychology) and have relevant work experience.

## Salaries

The salary that a psychologist can earn varies widely, depending on the type of work. The figures below offer some guidance, but actual rates will vary, depending on the type of work and the employer. There may also be regional variations, for example, most organisations (including the NHS, social services and government departments) offer higher rates of pay to those who work in London.

Psychologists working towards chartered psychologist status can expect to earn from £24,000 per annum during their training. Qualified psychologists can then expect to earn on scales that gradually rise to £40,000. Senior, experienced psychologists with responsibilities for departments or large specialist sections may earn up to £80,000.

The salaries of psychologists working in other roles vary widely. Others that do require further qualifications (such as university lecturers) might start on scales progressing from £25,000 to £38,000. Many of the posts in organisations (including social researchers, ergonomists and training and development officers) may not require further qualifications and might be on scales from £20,000 to £30,000. Psychologists in a third group (such as counsellors and police officers), who do require further qualifications and training but do not necessarily require degree status, also typically start on ranges from £20,000.

## Promotion

As you will have seen by looking at the description of salaries, the starting salary is not the only factor that you should consider. You also need to find out the salaries earned by more senior colleagues, and the chances that you will get promotion. For example, you could compare two roles that need postgraduate qualifications (typically at doctorate level) with one that needs only an undergraduate qualification.

- After training, a chartered psychologist can expect to earn in the range £29,000 to £40,000, and may get promotion to senior psychologist, perhaps earning up to £80,000.

- A university lecturer with a doctorate can expect to earn on a scale from £25,000 to £38,000, with the chance of promotion to senior lecturer earning up to £50,000.

- A consumer psychologist will typically earn in the range £18,000 to £24,000, but may get promotion to senior level and earn around £50,000.

## Other benefits

When comparing the various types of work, it's also important to consider other long-term benefits.

People working for the public sector (for example, the NHS, local authorities and government departments) generally have far greater job security than those working in the private sector.

Public sector workers usually also benefit from better pension arrangements. Most public sector workers (at least, in 2009) can expect to be paid an inflation-linked pension based on their final salary; this type of pension is rapidly becoming less common in the private sector.

On the other hand, workers in the private sector may be offered other benefits such as private health care insurance, use of sports facilities, and perhaps a company car.

# CHOOSING A CAREER

The following chapters of this book describe many careers open to psychologists. Before you study those chapters, spend a few minutes working out what you want from your career. Use the questions below to assess what you will have learned from completing a psychology degree, what working in a psychology-based job generally involves, and what skills and attributes you will need. Note that they are presented as checklists so that you can consider each point in turn and so identify any gaps in your skills, any aspects of the work that you would not enjoy, and any other issues.

## Working in psychology in practice

Although each field of psychology is different, they all involve working with other people and thinking about how they perceive, think, feel and act. The main tasks can generally be grouped under the following headings.

- Working with a wide range of clients.

- Working as part of a multi-disciplinary team.

- Using a range of methods to assess and diagnose problems and situations.

- Selecting and planning a suitable programme of treatment or development.

- Carrying out research.

## Generic skills

A psychology degree should give you a number of generic skills that can be used in many careers.

- Communication skills, including listening, speaking and writing.

- Numeracy and research skills, including collecting and analysing data and reporting on your findings.

- The ability to use information technology, including computer programs, the web and the Internet.

- The ability to work and learn independently, including self-motivation and time-management skills.

- The ability to work in teams, understand other people's viewpoints and influence others.

## Particular skills

The effective psychologist needs particular skills in:

- two-way communication with clients, colleagues and others in the organisation

- working both independently and as part of a team

- analysing each client's (or organisation's) situation and identifying possible ways of working towards solutions

- a particular aspect of psychology, and an understanding of when a colleague is better able to offer the skills required

- assessing possible ethical issues, for example, relating to confidentiality, equality and diversity

- designing research, carrying it out, analysing the findings and writing a report.

## Attributes

More general attributes needed for many careers in psychology include being:

- able to see situations from other people's point of view

- emotionally resilient, so that the clients' experiences do not affect your own life

- self-aware, understanding how your own behaviour and attitudes may affect clients and others in the organisation

- patient; many people (whether clients or team members) will only present their case slowly and it can often be a serious error to draw conclusions too soon

■   an effective team player, able to influence and motivate others

■   self-motivating, able to work independently, sometimes in difficult and challenging situations

■   intellectually rigorous, so that you can investigate and research issues scientifically and produce valid results.

## WHAT NEXT?

Working through this chapter will have highlighted that the range of careers available in psychology is very wide. Chapter 2 gives a summary of those possible careers, showing what each job involves, what you can expect to earn and what qualifications are generally required.

# Chapter Two
# CHOOSING A SPECIALISM

A psychology degree can qualify you for a very wide range of occupations. In fact, only about one-fifth of psychology graduates go on to work as professional psychologists. Others use their skills and knowledge in other areas of health and social care, in schools and universities, and in various roles in public sector and private sector organisations.

This chapter outlines many of the various careers, and the qualifications and experience you will need for each type of job. You'll see that people often follow different paths to get to the same job role, so making a decision now may not necessarily limit the choices open to you in the future. On the other hand, do note that some careers (such as clinical psychology or educational psychology) involve extended periods of training. A clinical psychologist will typically follow at least a three-year period of further training and study after graduating with a psychology degree.

Before deciding on a specialism, think also about getting some work experience in a related field before making a final decision. For example, you would be well advised to do some work as a care assistant or similar role in a residential mental health centre before committing yourself to a career working with people who have serious mental illness. Gaining experience coaching sports or leading sports teams is probably essential before you decide to apply for a course leading to qualifications in sport and exercise psychology.

# CATEGORISING CAREERS

In the later sections of this chapter you will find descriptions of nearly 50 careers, each of which can be followed by people with degrees in psychology or, in many cases, other qualifications such as HNDs, A-levels or previous experience.

Each of the careers has been classified under four main headings.

■ Health/social care.

■ Community work.

■ Education.

■ Organisational roles.

Each heading is then subdivided so that you can see what qualifications each career typically needs. For most headings there are subdivisions for careers that need a doctorate in psychology, need some other form of further qualification, or are suitable for new graduates or those with other qualifications. The descriptions of the qualifications required cannot possibly cover every possible route into the professions, so you may have to search or ask potential employers for more information if you have different experience or qualifications.

## Summarising the career options

All of these headings and subdivisions are shown in the figure on the opposite page. For example, you can see that a clinical psychologist role is in the 'health and social care' category and requires a doctorate in psychology. In contrast, looking in the 'organisational roles' category for jobs that are suitable for new graduates, you'll find that this may be sufficient qualification for a training and development officer.

The aim of the following chart is to show how the various careers can be categorised. It may appear confusing at first, but note that once you select a particular category like health and social care, you will then only have to consider a small section of the chart. Each small section is then repeated at the start of the discussion of careers in that particular category.

# Summarising the career options

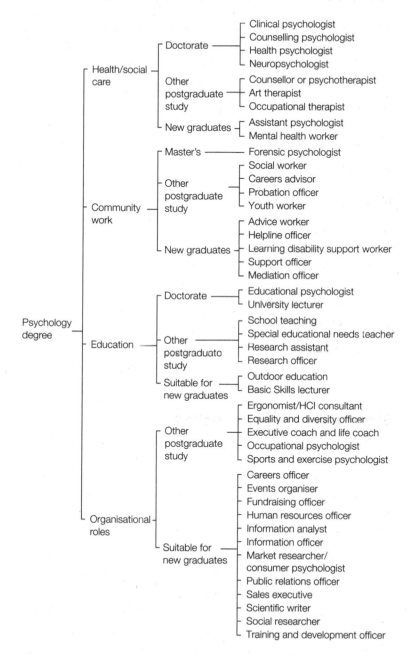

Psychology degree

**Health/social care**

- Doctorate
  - Clinical psychologist
  - Counselling psychologist
  - Health psychologist
  - Neuropsychologist
- Other postgraduate study
  - Counsellor or psychotherapist
  - Art therapist
  - Occupational therapist
- New graduates
  - Assistant psychologist
  - Mental health worker

**Community work**

- Master's
  - Forensic psychologist
- Other postgraduate study
  - Social worker
  - Careers advisor
  - Probation officer
  - Youth worker
- New graduates
  - Advice worker
  - Helpline officer
  - Learning disability support worker
  - Support officer
  - Mediation officer

**Education**

- Doctorate
  - Educational psychologist
  - University lecturer
- Other postgraduate study
  - School teaching
  - Special educational needs teacher
  - Research assistant
  - Research officer
- Suitable for new graduates
  - Outdoor education
  - Basic Skills lecturer

**Organisational roles**

- Other postgraduate study
  - Ergonomist/HCI consultant
  - Equality and diversity officer
  - Executive coach and life coach
  - Occupational psychologist
  - Sports and exercise psychologist
- Suitable for new graduates
  - Careers officer
  - Events organiser
  - Fundraising officer
  - Human resources officer
  - Information analyst
  - Information officer
  - Market researcher/consumer psychologist
  - Public relations officer
  - Sales executive
  - Scientific writer
  - Social researcher
  - Training and development officer

## Careers for psychologists

The term 'organisational roles' is used for posts in a range of organisations where a qualification in psychology will be useful but is not generally a requirement. For example, a human resources officer may work in a private or public sector organisation. If you have a psychology degree you will generally need to show that you have, or will work towards, further qualification in human resources.

The figure on the previous page is inevitably oversimplified and cannot show all the possible jobs or details of the qualifications and experience that may be required for each one. In particular, it cannot show some of the alternative ways in which people may become qualified for a particular job because of their life experience, work experience or qualifications in other subject areas. If you want to find out about the specific requirements for each career, you will need to refer to the websites of either the British Psychological Society (www.bps.org.uk) or Prospects (www.prospects.ac.uk).

# WHAT NEXT?

This chapter offers a very brief summary of each career and the qualifications that are typically needed. It does not give you enough information to make a final decision about your future career, but it should help you to choose a few possibilities.

If you have a particular interest in one or more of the various types of chartered psychologist, you can then study the specific information shown in Chapters 3 to 8.

Even if you do not want to go into a profession that requires chartered status, it may still help to study one or more of those chapters. For example, if you think you might want to train as a counsellor, much of the information in Chapter 3 (Clinical Psychology) will be highly relevant. Chapter 8 (Health, Sport and Exercise Psychology) is also highly relevant to all careers in the field of individual or community health.

If your interests do not relate closely to any of Chapters 3 to 8, then you should follow up the web links suggested in this chapter. Prospects (www.prospects.ac.uk) gives a great deal of specific information about particular careers and you could also try searching the web using the job title. You will very often find the website of a professional organisation representing people working in that career. For example, using the terms 'probation officer' gives access to many sites describing careers in the probation service, and to the National Association of Probation Officers.

Whichever of the above options you choose, you should then continue your study by reading Chapters 9 to 11. Chapter 9 gives more information about the various skills and attributes that you may need, and describes a variety of career paths that people may follow. Chapter 10 discusses the questions you need to ask before applying for your first job. And Chapter 11 helps you to look at long-term career planning: you may know where you want to be in a year's time, but what do you want to be doing 20 years (or 40 years!) from now?

# WORKING IN HEALTH AND SOCIAL CARE

Work in health and social care may be based in hospitals, primary care practices, prisons, charities, and public or private organisations. Most roles involve working with people who have problems that are psychologically based or are based on a physical disability or injury. The aims may be to work with the client so that the problem is reduced or removed, or may involve helping the individual to live as independently as possible.

Note that you can find out more about all of the roles in health and social care by searching for the specific job title on the www.nhscareers.nhs. uk website. The careers for psychologists in health and social care are shown below.

## Careers in health and social care

## Roles that need a doctorate/master's qualification and chartered status

Certain roles in the field of health and social care need postgraduate training leading to a doctorate or master's in a specific aspect of psychology. Most of these roles also require that you have been accepted as a chartered psychologist by the British Psychological Society (see Chapter 9).

## Clinical psychologist

Clinical psychologists work in a range of health settings with people who have psychologically based problems, such as addictions, depression, personality disorders or post-traumatic stress. The clinical psychologist's primary task is to assess clients and plan a treatment programme for them. They may also provide some types of psychological therapy and may carry out research, for example into the effectiveness of therapeutic treatments. Clinical psychology is described in more detail in Chapter 3.

## Counselling psychologist

Counselling psychologists work in a similar range of settings to clinical psychologists, providing psychological therapy for clients, perhaps following referral from a clinical psychologist. Counselling psychologists tend to follow one or more of the four broad approaches to therapy: psychodynamic; humanistic; cognitive behavioural; and systems or family therapy. You can find a brief summary of these approaches in Chapter 3.

## Health psychologist

Health psychologists work in hospitals and health authorities and rehabilitation centres. Their work focuses on two primary areas: promoting healthy living so as to prevent physical or mental illness; and working with people who have major physical illnesses or have experienced major accidents.

## Neuropsychologist

Neuropsychologists work with people who have suffered brain injury. This may involve people with an illness such as a stroke or Alzheimer's disease, people who have suffered injury as a result of an accident or assault, and people who have suffered from the effects of substance abuse. Neuropsychology is described in more detail in Chapter 3.

All of the above generally require a doctorate (or at least a master's) in the relevant area of psychology, extensive practical experience gained in relevant work before starting that course, and a 2:1 or better degree in a accredited psychology degree. See Chapter 9 for more details on these requirements.

## Roles that need other postgraduate study

Certain jobs need study on courses at certificate, diploma or master's level following a first degree in psychology.

## Counsellor or psychotherapist

Counsellors and psychotherapists provide psychological therapies to those experiencing addictions, depression, post-traumatic stress, anxiety and similar problems. They may work in primary care, for charities, for large organisations, schools or universities, or in private practice. Like counselling psychologists, counsellors and psychotherapists tend to follow one or more from the four broad approaches to therapy: psychodynamic; humanistic; cognitive behavioural; and systems or family therapy (see the brief summary of these approaches in Chapter 3).

There is some overlap between the uses of the two terms, but counsellors tend to work in short-term, solution-based ways, whereas psychotherapists are more likely to deal with more deep-rooted problems. To become an accredited counsellor or psychotherapist requires study on a course accredited by the British Association for Counselling and Psychotherapy (BACP) or the United Kingdom Council for Psychotherapy (UKCP).

## Art therapist

Art therapists use creative arts, such as art, music, drama or dance, to help people to explore their emotions. They may work with children or adults who have learning difficulties, autism, or have experienced trauma or head injuries. Art therapists generally work as members of a team in day centres, addiction clinics, special schools, prisons or hospices. They typically work with individuals or groups of clients referred by a clinical psychologist.

Qualification with the relevant body (e.g. the British Association for Art Therapists) requires postgraduate study in art therapy, some previous study in the selected art, and practical experience of working in mental health or social care.

## Occupational therapist

Occupational therapists work with clients and their carers to help the individual to live as independently as possible. Typical clients include those with mental health problems, disabled children or adults and their families, and those who have experienced major injuries. Occupational therapists may be based in hospitals, large primary care practices or rehabilitation centres, though their work will often involve visiting clients in their homes.

Registration as an occupational therapist requires a postgraduate diploma or master's qualification. Acceptance onto such a course is more likely if you have some relevant work experience.

### Roles suitable for newly qualified graduates

Certain jobs may be open to new graduates, though the chances of getting the job will be increased by having suitable work experience or having completed other, relevant training.

## Assistant psychologist

Assistant psychologists may assist some of the various chartered psychologists listed in the previous group, for example, clinical and forensic psychologists. For details of what each role may involve, you should study the preceding descriptions of the various types of chartered psychologist. Do note that assistant psychologist posts are very popular, as they are attractive to people who are looking for work experience before applying for a doctorate in psychology courses.

## Mental health worker

Mental health workers provide specialist services in primary care settings (typically linked to a GP surgery) for people with mental health needs.

They tend to use relatively short-term approaches, such as cognitive behavioural therapy or anxiety management, to work with clients with mild to moderate mental health problems.

Mental health workers may be psychology graduates or may come from a range of other backgrounds, including nursing and social work. On appointment, workers study for a one-year part-time course, the Postgraduate Certificate in Mental Health.

### Mental health policy officer

Mental health policy officers may work in a variety of government organisations and health agencies. Rather than working with individual clients, they focus on analysing the current provision of mental health services and devising ways of improving or building on these.

While a psychology degree may be sufficient, the chances of getting a post as a mental health policy officer are greatly increased if you have experience of working in the mental health field and if you have further qualifications involving research. For more on the work of a typical body working in this field, see the website of the National Institute for Mental Health in England (http://nimhe.csip.org.uk).

## COMMUNITY WORK

The range of opportunities for psychology graduates in the various areas of community work is very wide. Some of these are summarised below, and you will also find suggested sources of further information.

## Careers in community work

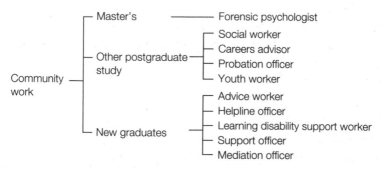

# Roles that need a doctorate/master's qualification and chartered status

## Forensic psychologist

Forensic psychologists work with psychological aspects of the law, working with the police, the prison system, or in university or government research. For example, they may apply psychological theories to criminal investigations, criminal behaviour and the treatment of criminals. In the media you may see forensic psychologists referred to as 'profilers', 'criminal psychologists' or 'criminologists'. Forensic psychology is described in more detail in Chapter 6.

# Roles that need other postgraduate study

Certain jobs need study on courses at certificate, diploma or master's level following a first degree in psychology.

## Social worker

Social workers are employed by local authorities to work with individuals and families in crisis or who are experiencing social exclusion. Mental health social workers are employed by various NHS organisations to work specifically with those with mental health problems. The work may be carried out in day care centres, hospitals or in the client's home.

Psychology graduates will need to follow a two-year master's degree in social work that has been approved by the General Social Care Council (GSCC). The course involves a combination of theory and 200 days spent in practice settings where you will gain practical experience. For further information, see www.socialworkandcare.co.uk.

## Careers advisor

Careers advisors generally work with young people through the government's Connexions support service, or for school or university careers departments. Depending on the work situation, they may also provide guidance on financial and housing issues.

It is generally useful, though not essential, to have followed a postgraduate course in careers guidance. For further information, see the Institute of Careers Guidance (www.icg-uk.org).

## Probation officer

Probation officers work with offenders and the courts. The work may involve making assessment of offenders before they are sentenced, ensuring that they comply with court orders, and working to rehabilitate offenders and successfully reintegrate them into the community.

Psychology graduates can qualify as probation officers through a two-year postgraduate course in probation studies (or, in Northern Ireland, in social work). This course combines theoretical study with practical, on-the-job work experience. For information on the National Probation Service, see www.probation.homeoffice.gov.uk.

## Youth worker

Youth workers may work in schools, colleges, youth centres, faith-based centres or voluntary organisations. They typically organise activities for young people and help them to develop skills and deal with personal issues.

A psychology degree and relevant experience may qualify a person for a youth worker post, but it is often useful to have a specific further postgraduate qualification validated by the National Youth Agency or the Youth Council for Northern Ireland. For further information on careers in youth work, see the National Youth Agency website (www. nya.org.uk).

## Roles suitable for newly qualified graduates

Certain jobs may be open to new graduates, though the chances of getting the job will be increased by having suitable work experience or having completed other, relevant training.

## Advice worker

Advice workers may be generalists or may work in specific fields, such as welfare rights, employment for disabled people, immigration issues, homelessness, drug dependency or legal matters. As one example, housing advisors work with those at risk of losing their homes, people in dispute with the landlord, the homeless, and people with special housing needs.

Advisors may be employed by local authorities, charities or advice centres. A psychology degree and relevant work experience are useful qualifications, and initial on-the-job training is given. For information on the various advisory organisations, see www.adviceuk.org.uk.

## Helpline officer, learning disability support worker, support officer

A number of roles of this type are available in local authorities. They do not need a degree qualification but may be suitable for graduates who are looking for relevant work experience before they study for further qualifications in social work.

## Mediation officer

Mediation officers work in a number of areas of dispute, for example, working with families where there is a risk of a young person becoming homeless, or working with couples experiencing marital difficulties.

Mediation officers may be employed by local authorities, charities or private organisations. A psychology degree and relevant work experience are useful qualifications, and initial on-the-job training is generally given. It is also useful to have followed courses on mediation or conflict resolution. For information on family mediation, see the UK College of Family Mediation website (www.ukcfm.co.uk).

## Police officer

Police officers tackle antisocial behaviour, aim to reduce robbery and street crime, combat organised crime and terrorism, support victims and provide a reassuring presence in the community.

While a degree is not a requirement for selection, the knowledge and skills gained will be beneficial. All successful candidates do have to satisfy job-related fitness and medical tests. A High Potential Development Scheme in England, Wales and Northern Ireland is designed to develop the future leaders of the police service. There is an Accelerated Promotion Scheme for graduates in Scotland. For more on careers in the police force, see www.police-information.co.uk.

# EDUCATION

There is a wide range of opportunities for psychology graduates in the various areas of education. Some of these are summarised below, and you will also find suggested sources of further information.

## Careers in education

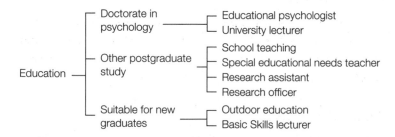

## Roles that need a doctorate qualification

Certain roles in education generally need postgraduate training for three years leading to a doctorate in a specific aspect of psychology. Some of these roles also require that the person has been accepted as a chartered psychologist by the British Psychological Society (see Chapter 0).

## Educational psychologist

Educational psychologists work to help children and young people in the education system. They may work with the child, the school and the family, dealing primarily with difficulties in learning or social adjustment. Educational psychologists generally work for the local education authority.

To become an educational psychologist you need to follow a three-year course leading to a Doctorate in Educational Psychology and gain chartered status through the British Psychological Society (see Chapter 9). Educational psychology is described in more detail in Chapter 4.

## University lecturer

Psychology lecturers work with undergraduate and postgraduate students in universities and colleges in departments such as psychology, education, management, medicine or nursing. The work involves planning, teaching and assessing courses, supporting students and carrying out the related administrative work. They are also expected to carry out their own research, publish their findings and seek financial support for future projects.

At university level, a postgraduate qualification is virtually essential. Lecturers may choose to gain accreditation as a Chartered Teaching and Research Psychologist through the British Psychological Society (see www.bps.org.uk).

## Roles that need other postgraduate study

Certain jobs need study on courses at certificate, diploma or master's level following a first degree in psychology.

## School teaching

As well as time spent teaching in the classroom, teachers spend considerable time preparing lessons, marking and discussing children's progress. Teachers in primary schools teach a wide range of subjects, whereas teachers in secondary schools tend to focus on one or two.

Teachers must have a postgraduate certificate in education. Psychology graduates will generally need another specialist subject if they wish to teach in secondary schools. You can find out more from the Department for Children, Schools and Families (www.dcsf.gov.uk/index.htm).

## Special educational needs teacher

The term 'special educational needs' is applied to children who have learning difficulties, emotional or behavioural problems, some form of disability or are exceptionally gifted. They may be taught individually or in small groups in special schools, within special units in other schools, or in community homes, hospital schools or youth custody centres.

Special educational needs teachers must have a Postgraduate Certificate in Education and will normally also need to have had at least two years of teaching experience in the classroom. You can find out more from the National Association for Special Educational Needs (www.nasen.org.uk) or the Department for Children, Schools and Families (www.dcsf.gov.uk/index.htm).

## Research assistant, research officer

Many chartered psychologists, and others, carry out research as part of their work. Research assistants and research officers work solely on research in universities, government bodies and the NHS.

Research assistants generally need to have a psychology degree and a master's or doctorate that shows some evidence of having carried out independent research. It is also useful to have had some practical experience in the mental health field. For further information, see the British Psychological Society website (www.bps.org.uk), searching for the sections on teachers and researchers.

## Roles suitable for newly qualified graduates

A number of other roles In education may be of interest to people with psychology degrees. Examples include work in outdoor education or in Basic Skills work in a further education (FE) college. Do note, however, that these will need further training and qualifications in, for example, canoeing, mountain safety, or in planning Basic Skills programmes for someone recovering from a head injury.

# ORGANISATIONAL ROLES

Both public and private sector organisations offer many opportunities for psychology graduates. For example, a company or a government department may employ psychologists to work in human resources, health and safety, and training roles. Some of the most common roles are summarised below, and you will also find suggested sources of further information.

## Careers in organisational roles

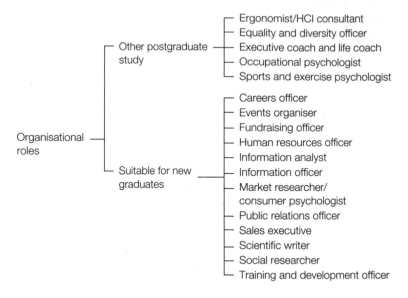

Organisational roles
- Other postgraduate study
  - Ergonomist/HCI consultant
  - Equality and diversity officer
  - Executive coach and life coach
  - Occupational psychologist
  - Sports and exercise psychologist
- Suitable for new graduates
  - Careers officer
  - Events organiser
  - Fundraising officer
  - Human resources officer
  - Information analyst
  - Information officer
  - Market researcher/consumer psychologist
  - Public relations officer
  - Sales executive
  - Scientific writer
  - Social researcher
  - Training and development officer

## Roles that need other postgraduate study

Certain jobs need study on courses at certificate, diploma or master's level following a first degree in psychology.

### Ergonomist and human–computer interaction consultant

Ergonomists investigate the ways in which people use equipment and machines, plan how they can use them safely and most effectively, and write related reports and procedures. In a similar way human–computer interaction consultants study how people use computers, both in terms of the physical equipment and the software. Ergonomists and human–computer interaction consultants may work for large companies, or may work as consultants to, for example, telecommunications companies and entertainment companies.

Entry to the profession can be gained with a psychology degree and a master's or doctorate in an ergonomics course recognised by the

Ergonomics Society, or a human–computer interaction course in a university computing department. Employers favour candidates with industrial experience, and around one-third of new entrants have had experience in another occupation. For further information, see the website of the Ergonomics Society (www.ergonomics.org.uk) or Interaction (www.bcs-hci.org.uk).

## Equality and diversity officer

Equality and diversity officers work to ensure equality and diversity within organisations, and to promote the benefits of those policies. The work will typically be within the human resources department, and will relate to recruitment, selection, pay and conditions, training and development, and promotion. It typically involves analysing the organisation's performance, ensuring that managers and others follow the relevant procedures, and devising new systems and processes.

A psychology degree gives useful insights on people in the workplace, but candidates will often need to show evidence of further study in this field. This could be through a postgraduate diploma or master's level course, or could involve qualification through the Chartered Institute of Personnel and Development. See www.diversitylink.co.uk for further information, with its many examples of recruitment advertisements giving information on organisations' requirements.

## Executive coach and life coach

The term 'life coaching' is used to describe working with individual clients to help them to set their own goals and work to achieve them. It is an unregulated field where qualifications can be gained through work with private training providers.

Psychology graduates who wish to gain a more formal qualification can enrol on a coaching and mentoring postgraduate certificate, diploma or master's. Jobs will generally be offered with human resources departments of large private organisations. Further details on coaching can be found in the Special Group in Coaching Psychology section of the British Psychological Society (www.bps.org.uk).

## Occupational psychologist

Occupational psychologists work to improve individual, team and organisational performance. They focus on the interactions between work conditions and tasks and people's well-being, motivation and performance. Occupational psychologists also identify and resolve issues relating to, for example, team culture, training, and health and safety.

To gain accreditation by the British Psychological Society, students must complete a psychology degree and a master's in occupational psychology. To gain chartered psychologist status, the student must then complete two years of supervised work experience (see Chapter 9). For further information, see the British Psychological Society website (www.bps.org.uk).

## Sports and exercise psychologist

Sports and exercise psychologists use their understanding of psychology to help individuals to improve their performance. They may be employed by sports clubs, sports centres, universities or health promotion programmes.

To gain accreditation by the British Psychological Society, students must complete a psychology degree and master's in sport and exercise psychology. To gain chartered psychologist status, the student must then complete two years of supervised work experience (see Chapter 9). For further information on sports and exercise psychology, see the British Psychological Society website (www.bps.org.uk).

## Roles suitable for newly qualified graduates

A number of jobs in organisational roles may be open to new graduates, though the chances of getting the job will be increased by having suitable work experience or having completed other, relevant training.

## Careers officer

Careers officers work in a wide range of organisations, including universities, human resources departments of organisations, government agencies and the forces. The aims are to provide information and to help individuals to understand their own motivations and options and so select a suitable future career step.

See also the description of the careers advisor role, generally involving work with young people through the government's Connexions support service, in the section on community work.

It is generally useful, though not essential, to have followed a postgraduate course in careers guidance. For further information, see the Institute of Careers Guidance (www.icg-uk.org).

## Events organiser

Events organisers are responsible for organising exhibitions, conferences, festivals, fundraising and social events. The work may involve researching venues, planning programmes, working with exhibitors and venues, and generally co-ordinating all aspects of the event. They may work for large organisations, or for consultancies that arrange events.

Candidates with a first degree may be accepted onto a graduate training scheme within the organisation, or may be encouraged to follow training courses after they have started work. Alternatively, you could study for a postgraduate certificate, diploma or master's qualification in marketing or market research before looking for your first job. For further details, see the websites of the Chartered Institute of Marketing (www.cim.co.uk) or the Communication Advertising and Marketing Education Foundation (www.camfoundation.com).

## Fundraising officer

Fundraising officers work in charities, universities, the NHS and similar organisations to raise money from corporate and private donors. This may be done, for example, through direct mailing, telephone campaigns, corporate sponsorship or charity events.

A psychology degree gives useful insights into how people may react to fundraising techniques. Candidates with a first degree may be accepted onto a graduate training scheme within a large organisation, or may be encouraged to work towards qualification through the Institute of Fundraising (www.institute-of-fundraising.org.uk).

## Human resources officer

Human resources (HR) officers work on the recruitment, pay and conditions, training and development of people in an organisation. The role can be seen as a link between the business needs of the organisation and its managers and the financial and social needs of the employees.

A psychology degree gives useful insights on people in the workplace. Candidates with a first degree may be accepted onto a graduate training scheme within the organisation, or may be encouraged to work towards qualification through the Chartered Institute of Personnel and Development (www.cipd.co.uk). Alternatively, you could choose to study for a master's or a diploma in HR management.

## Information analyst

Information analysts collect and analyse large quantities of data, presenting the information and conclusions in written reports. They may work for the NHS, university researchers, government departments or large private organisations.

Many of the skills will have been learned as part of a research and analysis element of a psychology degree. No further formal qualification will generally be required, though applicants will benefit if they can show some previous relevant work experience and some knowledge of the relevant computer analysis tools. For information on a range of careers involving analysis of data, see the website of the Royal Statistical Society (www.rss.org.uk).

## Information officer

Information officers manage the vast amount of information available to organisations and direct it, or make it available, to the most relevant people. This typically involves using online databases and Internet resources, as well as traditional library materials. They may work in various levels of government, libraries, the health service, education, media organisations, the financial and legal sectors, and in non-governmental organisations.

Many of the skills will have been learned as part of a research and analysis element of a psychology degree. No further formal qualification will generally be required and many organisations provide on-the-job training. Some organisations require a postgraduate diploma or master's in a course accredited by the Chartered Institute of Library and Information Professionals (www.cilip.org.uk).

## Market researcher and consumer psychologist

Market researchers collect data on behalf of organisations such as businesses, governments and charities, and provide information that can be used when making future marketing decisions. Researchers may use a range of techniques including questionnaires, electronic data collection, focus groups and interviews.

Consumer psychologists work within commercial and public organisations to study the behaviour and preferences of actual and potential customers. They present reports on their findings, which are then used by the organisation to plan its future marketing.

Candidates with a first degree may be accepted onto a graduate training scheme within the organisation, or may be encouraged to follow training courses after they have started work. Alternatively, you could study for a postgraduate certificate, diploma or master's qualification in marketing or market research before looking for your first job. For further details, see the websites of the Chartered Institute of Marketing (www.cim.co.uk) and the Market Research Society (www.mrs.org.uk).

## Public relations officer

Public relations (PR) officers aim to manage the reputation of their organisation. They work with newspapers, television, radio and the web to create a suitable image of the organisation. Public relations officers may work for private organisations or public ones like the NHS and universities, or charities.

A degree is a useful, though not essential, qualification for work in PR. The Chartered Institute of Public Relations is currently piloting a new qualification – the Introductory Award in Public Relations. For further details, see the Chartered Institute of Public Relations website (www. cipr.co.uk).

## Sales executive

Sales executives aim to maximise the long-term sales of a product or service by developing and maintaining relationships with customers. They work closely with marketing staff to build and maintain the company's market.

A psychology degree is a useful, though not essential, qualification for work in sales. On-the-job training is generally provided, and some organisations have graduate training schemes.

## Scientific writer

A degree course in psychology provides useful training in analysing information and presenting summaries and conclusions. These skills form a useful foundation for a future career in scientific writing, producing written materials for newspapers, magazines, journals, industrial or service companies, or government agencies.

The chance of finding work in scientific writing will be greatly increased if you have some specific training and work experience. There are a number of suitable postgraduate certificate, diploma or master's level courses in journalism. See the Association of British Science Writers website (www.absw.org.uk).

## Social researcher

Social researchers can use the skills and knowledge gained from a psychology degree to carry out social research for government departments and agencies, local authorities and the NHS, or charities. Examples of topics for research include the effects of ageing, crime, health care, transport and unemployment. The work involves collecting and analysing data, drawing conclusions and reporting the findings.

A psychology degree may be sufficient qualification for a post as a social researcher. However, your chances of appointment will be greater if you have a postgraduate diploma or master's in social research. For further information see the Government Social Research website (www.gsr.gov.uk).

## Training and development officer

Training and development officers plan, and may deliver, training within public and private organisations. The work will often involve identifying training needs and planning suitable programmes with internal and external training providers. Finally, the officer will need to devise ways of assessing the effectiveness of training programmes.

A psychology degree may be sufficient qualification for a post as a training and development officer. However, a master's or diploma recognised by the Chartered Institute of Personnel and Development will improve your chances (see www.cipd.co.uk).

# Chapter Three
# CLINICAL PSYCHOLOGY

Clinical psychologists generally work in the health service, often working in partnership with other health professionals and social workers. They work with a range of clients who are experiencing psychologically based problems, such as addiction, depression, personality disorders or post-traumatic stress.

As a clinical psychologist you would generally work through a three-stage process starting with assessing the client. You would then diagnose the problem and devise a treatment plan. Finally, you might either work therapeutically with clients or might refer them to a more suitable professional. Clinical psychologists are often also expected to carry out research, for example into the effectiveness of different therapies.

The work is challenging, sometimes involving working with difficult or abusive clients. On the other hand, there are great rewards in seeing the benefits of therapy for clients. You'll work with a team of dedicated professionals, but also have considerable freedom about organising your own time and work.

If you think clinical psychology might be for you, this chapter describes the work in some detail and then explains what qualifications and training you will need. It ends with a summary of what the work involves, of the 'highs' and 'lows' that you might expect, and checklists that you can use to assess whether you have the relevant attributes and skills.

# WHAT DO CLINICAL PSYCHOLOGISTS DO?

## Examples from a case load

To get an idea of the work of a clinical psychologist, have a look at some of the very brief scenarios below.

- Andy and Bina have been married for 20 years. It was all fine at first, but now the family spends all its time arguing. Andy thinks the problem is caused by their son, Carl, and suspects he's taking drugs. Carl says that Andy is always picking on him and his mother.

- Deepak's a teenager who always seems to get in trouble, at home, in school and in the evenings and weekends. He seems to think everyone hates him, so tends to hit out at anyone who says anything critical.

- Evelyn's been alternately bingeing on food and dieting for four years. Her GP is convinced that Evelyn's problem is linked to arguments with her husband after a miscarriage.

- Frank suffered minor brain damage in a car accident and can no longer work. At 30, he is becoming depressed at the prospect of never working again and says that there's really no point in living.

- Gordon is 95 and is convinced that he can live on his own provided he gets some support with washing and meals. The local social services department is concerned about him. They consider that he is at risk to himself when no carer is present, but Gordon strongly disagrees.

Those five cases are all typical of people and situations that a clinical psychologist could meet. As you can see, they're pretty varied, so will need a variety of skills and knowledge. More important, none of them can be solved by simply telling each person what to do: clinical psychologists have to work with people to decide what will best relieve their distress and enable them to function and feel better about themselves.

## Clinical psychology in more detail

Clinical psychologists use theoretical knowledge to understand, prevent and relieve psychologically based distress or dysfunction. The aim is to promote subjective well-being and personal development.

To look at that definition in more detail we first need to look at what is meant by 'psychologically based distress or dysfunction'. It's probably easiest to think of examples, such as addiction, anorexia, bulimia, sleep difficulties, sexual problems, clinical depression, anxiety, mental illness, phobias, or trauma following an accident or abuse. All of these examples of distress or dysfunction could be prevented or relieved by the work of the clinical psychologist.

The clinical psychologist will work with the client or clients to encourage self-development: the aim is to help the person to change their behaviour and their view of themselves. It's important to note the aim of working towards 'subjective well-being'. Clinical psychologists are generally interested in helping people to change their views, lifestyles or actions so that the individuals feel better about themselves.

The final part of the definition that we need to consider is the idea of 'using theoretical knowledge to understand, prevent and relieve' distress or dysfunction. The work of the clinical psychologist must be based on a sound theoretical approach (the four most commonly used approaches are described in a later section).

The psychologist will typically follow a three-stage process of assessment, diagnosis and then working with the client to encourage new ways of thinking, feeling or behaving. In many cases, it may be that the work with the client must be referred to a colleague. Thinking again of the case examples listed at the start of the chapter, the psychologist might decide that the family's problem is caused by Carl's drug habit and refer Carl to a drug counsellor; or it may be that the problem seems to be linked to the family in general, in which case it could be more suitable to refer them to a family therapist.

## Specific areas of work

To get a more detailed idea of the different areas in which a clinical psychologist may work, have a look at the following list. It shows the placements available to students of a Doctorate in Clinical Psychology (DClinPsy) at Bangor University at the time of writing this book. Students attending the course get clinical experience by working in various placements during their three-year studies.

- Adult mental health

- Older adults

- Children and adolescents

- Learning disabilities

- Forensic psychology

- Neuropsychology

- Palliative care

- Behavioural medicine (adults)

- Behavioural medicine (children)

- Primary care services for children

- Continuing care

- Adult survivors of sexual abuse

- Severe and enduring mental health problems

- Child development

- Childhood autism

- Child conduct disorder

- In-patient adolescents

- Challenging behaviour (learning disability)

- Profound learning disability.

## Work settings

Clinical psychologists work mainly in hospitals, psychiatric units, health centres, community mental health teams, child and adolescent mental health services, and social services. They generally work as part of a team including social workers, medical practitioners, occupational therapists and other health professionals. In this way, each client can be offered the most suitable therapies and support.

The teams in England and Wales are usually organised within NHS trusts or care trusts (partnerships between NHS trusts and local authorities). In Scotland, there are acute and primary care trusts for each health board area. In Northern Ireland, health and social services are co-ordinated by four health and social services boards, making it easier to forge links between the work of the different professionals.

Those clinical psychologists who work in the National Health Service can follow a clearly defined career structure. They may also choose to combine NHS work with research work, teaching or training.

Other clinical psychologists work in the private sector or may be self-employed. For example, there are jobs in private health schemes and universities. Large companies may appoint clinical psychologists to work with the distressed in their organisation, or to advise on recruitment, training and the development of good working relationships.

## Assessment and diagnosis

You saw earlier that clinical psychologists start their work with assessment and diagnosis. Only then do they work with clients or refer them to other professionals in the team.

Assessment may involve a number of techniques, such as:

- psychological and neuropsychological tests carried out by the psychologist

- self-reports completed by the client, for example giving ratings on a range of scales

- structured observations where the psychologist asks the client to carry out various tasks and observes how he or she performs them

- interviews with clients, their families or people involved in their care.

## Clinical or counselling psychology?

As you've seen from the descriptions above, after the assessment and diagnosis process the clinical psychologist will often refer the client to other professionals. One option is to refer to a counselling psychologist. This person will often have very similar qualifications to a clinical psychologist, but the focus of their work will be on the work with the client. In practice, the boundaries between the two professions are blurred, and many clinical psychologists will also act as counselling psychologists and vice versa.

## Four approaches

When working with clients, clinical psychologists generally follow an approach based on one of four theoretical approaches.

The **psychodynamic** approach primarily aims to make the client aware of his or her own unconscious drives. The student who reacts badly to male lecturers may be doing so because of unconscious memories of childhood mistreatment by a male; the woman who is afraid to leave the home may be reacting to having been sent to boarding school at an early age. This approach also focuses on the idea of transference: the client may transfer feelings about a significant person onto the psychologist. Psychologists working in this way thus need a particularly clear understanding of how they appear to others and how they may themselves react in various situations.

**Humanistic** psychologists, in contrast, focus on trying to show that they empathise with the client's feelings. The aim is to show 'unconditional positive regard' for the person and so help them to build a stronger personality and self-concept. Working with a sex offender the psychologist will try to show positive regard of the individual (though not of their actions); in this way the client may build a better self-concept, feel less alienated from society, and become less likely to offend in future.

**Cognitive behavioural** psychologists focus on the links between how we think ('cognition'), how we feel and how we act ('behaviour'). Working with a compulsive hand-washer, the aim will be to identify what thoughts are causing the compulsive behaviour. It may then be possible to break the links between those thoughts and the hand-washing.

**Systems** or **family** therapy involves working with groups of people, such as couples and families. The key is to look at the relationships and the ways in which a change by one person will affect the other group members. For example, scapegoating can occur if one son is being blamed for all the family's troubles. How can the psychologist help the family members to communicate better with him and between themselves, and how can they all start to view the son differently?

In practice, there are many variants on those four approaches, and some psychologists may use more than one approach. But every psychologist must base his or her work on a clear theoretical framework that enables them to follow a systematic process when assessing, diagnosing and working with the client.

Finally, clinical psychology is not the same as psychiatry. Both of them have similar primary aims: to reduce or remove mental distress or dysfunction. But psychiatrists are doctors with medical degrees and training, and generally focus on using medication to reduce or remove symptoms or causes of mental illness. Clinical psychologists, in contrast, focus on assessing and diagnosing the client so that they can choose suitable treatment and support from a wide range of options.

## Research

Clinical psychologists are also expected to carry out their own research, generally into the effectiveness of particular therapeutic treatments or other aspects of the help provided for clients. Most psychologists will carry out this research independently so need to have a good theoretical background and experience in designing and implementing research projects.

Research of various types is an important part of every Doctorate in Clinical Psychology course, and trainees are expected to have a good grounding in research methods if they are to be accepted onto such a course.

# ENTRY REQUIREMENTS

All clinical psychologists need to have a Doctorate in Clinical Psychology from an accredited course.

To be accepted for a three-year doctorate course, you will generally need at least a 2:1 degree in a relevant subject, be able to show that you have research skills and show that you have carried out relevant work experience.

If you have a 2:2 you will normally need to take a relevant master's course before you can be considered for a DClinPsy course. The master's should involve direct patient contact, and the collection of psychological data relating to clinical problems. A taught master's course would only be suitable if it had a strong emphasis on research methods.

You also need the Graduate Basis for Registration (GBR) of the British Psychological Society (BPS). Only certain accredited psychology degrees will make you eligible for GBR; others may only make you eligible for Graduate Membership of the BPS. Graduate Membership does not make you eligible for a DClinPsy course and you will need to take a conversion course or a qualifying examination. To find out which degree courses are accredited, and for more on conversion courses and qualifying examinations, see Chapter 9 or the careers section of the British Psychological Society website (www.bps.org.uk).

It is very competitive to gain a place on DClinPsy courses – fewer than 30% of applicants are successful each year. If successful, however, candidates become 'trainee clinical psychologists' and are generally employed by a local NHS trust. A large part of every course involves working in placements to gain practical experience.

## Studying psychology at university and school

If you are currently studying at school or college and think you may later wish to become a clinical psychologist, it's worth thinking in advance about how you could most easily progress towards that profession.

Studying psychology at GCSE or A-level will give you a good idea of the basics of the subject. It is also a useful preparation for almost any degree, particularly in subjects such as medicine, the sciences and social sciences. A-level psychology is not a requirement if you want to study the subject at university, though it will be useful. Whatever subjects you choose, however, do remember that you may need to show at least some understanding of the use of scientific methods.

When selecting a psychology course at university, remember that not all of them will give you Graduate Basis for Registration (GBR) of the British Psychological Society (BPS). If you think you may want to work as a clinical psychologist in the future, it is important to apply only for accredited courses.

## Mature students

Since acceptance for training as a clinical psychologist places such an emphasis on previous experience, it is quite common for mature students to study on DClinPsy courses. Thinking of the four approaches, you will also realise that some degree of maturity and self-knowledge is needed for many aspects of clinical psychology work.

If you are thinking of applying as a mature student but are unsure about whether your experience and qualifications are suitable, it will be worthwhile contacting the relevant university to find out whether or not particular experience in, say, nursing or social services is relevant.

## Work experience

As you can see from the box below, relevant experience is very important when applying for DClinPsy courses. If you refer to specific courses, you may find that that they lay down more specific requirements or give advice on how to go about gaining experience.

### University requirements relating to experience

'All trainees accepted onto the Programme will have had a minimum of six months' previous experience in a relevant field (e.g. research, learning difficulties, mental health, social services or the voluntary sector).' (Leeds University)

'Relevant experience which allows the applicant to apply psychological principles to practice is essential. Experience of applying and/or disseminating research is desirable. Previous working contact with, and supervision by, a clinical psychologist is an advantage, but other relevant work (e.g. nursing, support work) will be considered. Experience working on a clinically focused research project would also be seen as relevant, particularly if it involved direct client contact. A good range and amount of relevant experience is an advantage; however, it is more important to demonstrate an ability to reflect how this relates to clinical training and to the role of the clinical psychologist.' (Edinburgh University)

'We are interested in graduate applicants with... experience in a clinically relevant setting at the time of entry to the course, for example as an Assistant Psychologist, a Research Assistant on a clinically relevant project or having completed a clinically relevant PhD. Applicants with experience of other social, health care or research posts will also be considered. Lack of any direct experience in the NHS may be a disadvantage.' (Royal Holloway, University of London)

For links to these and other university prospectuses, see the Clearing House for Postgraduate Courses in Clinical Psychology, www.leeds.ac.uk/chpccp/index.html.

## International applicants

By applying for a clinical psychology training course you are also applying for a job with the NHS. That means you must have a right to work in the UK on a long-term basis. Citizens of the UK and the European Economic Area are generally eligible to work for the NHS long term and so can be accepted for training.

However, people from other countries would need to apply for a work permit, and cannot guarantee that they will be allowed to work in the UK for long periods. As a result they cannot usually be considered for DClinPsy courses.

## John is a clinical psychologist specialising in working with people with learning disabilities.

'When I was at school I did a lot of sport and was quite successful. I could never understand how some very skilful people seemed unable to play effectively in a team. In individual sports like tennis, I also had trouble understanding how a less skilful player could often win against a better opponent.

I decided to study psychology at university with the idea of becoming a sports psychologist.

'At university, I met students who were interested in working with people with what seemed to me to be more serious problems than how to win at tennis. Almost by chance I worked on a summer project providing holidays for people with learning disabilities. Since the organisation had its base near the university, I then got involved in evening and weekend work for them and gradually realised that I could continue this work by training as a clinical psychologist.

'After my first degree, I took a year out from study and found work as a research assistant in a local hospital. The work related mainly to elderly people with dementia, but it gave me useful ideas on how research is carried out in practice, and how the results of research can be used.

'I was accepted for a course leading to a Doctorate in Clinical Psychology, after a rather nerve-wracking interview process. They seemed quite pleased by my experience of research and of working with disabled people, but seemed a bit concerned about whether I would have trouble dealing with the inevitable frustrations that both the clients and their carers feel. I suppose I was a bit concerned too. When you only work with people for short periods you can always think, "It's alright, I'll be back at university or wherever soon."

'During the course, I carried out a research project into the possible effects on carers of having long periods without respite. I'm not sure whether the outcomes were particularly useful, but it certainly gave me insight into what it must be like to care for someone full-time.

'I've been working for five years now since qualifying. I'm based in a local hospital but do have to do quite a lot of travelling around to the various places where there is support for people with learning difficulties. I also sometimes visit people in their homes and have meetings with various local providers and charities. In many ways the work is satisfying, seeing the benefits that even quite simple changes can make. But there are frustrations: you always know that more could be done if there was more generous funding.

'What will I do next? I'm not sure. I suppose that I ought to think about going one step up the career ladder, but that could mean that I have less contact with individual clients, so I'll probably stay where I am for a little while.'

# IS THIS THE CAREER FOR ME?

## The practicalities

The work can be stressful since it often involves contact with people who are distressed in some way. On rare occasions, this may involve some level of personal risk. It's essential for all clinical psychologists to have a personal supervisor with whom they discuss cases and their reactions to them, and from whom they can gain support.

The working hours are mainly nine to five, but some evening and weekend work may be involved, for example to enable working people to attend a meeting or consultation. It may be necessary to be available on call in case of emergencies.

Most positions exist in large towns and cities, with fewer opportunities in rural areas. The psychologist will typically have to travel locally to attend meetings or meet colleagues.

Part-time working is common and positions with the NHS may allow other self-employment or freelance work. For example, a psychologist may set up a private clinical practice, or combine NHS work with industrial or commercial consultancy.

## Career prospects

While studying for a doctorate, trainee clinical psychologists are paid on NHS scale 6, starting at approximately £24,000 per annum. Qualified psychologists move to scale 7, a scale that currently (2009) runs from about £29,000 to £38,000. Senior, experienced psychologists with responsibilities for departments or large specialist sections may earn in the range of £44,000 to £80,000.

At present (2009) the career prospects for clinical psychologists are very good, with a number of vacancies. It's also likely that there will be long-term growth in the provision of psychological and social support, particularly for the increasing proportion of elderly people in the UK population.

## Self-assessment

In the following sections are brief descriptions of what the job is like in practice, what particular skills and attributes you'll need, and what clinical psychologists find particularly good (and bad) about their work. The comments have deliberately been kept brief so that you can use them as a checklist and assess whether you would suit this career, and whether it would suit you.

## The work in practice

The main tasks are:

- working with a wide range of people who are distressed or dysfunctional, and may have mental health problems

- working as part of a multi-disciplinary team typically including psychiatrists, medical practitioners, counselling psychologists, psychotherapists and social workers

- using a range of methods to assess and diagnose the problems being experienced by a range of clients

- selecting and planning a suitable programme of treatment for each client, often involving work with other professionals

- carrying out therapeutic work with clients, where there is a match between the client's needs and the psychologist's skills and experience

- carrying out research, generally into the effectiveness of particular therapeutic methods or systems.

## Skills and attributes

The effective clinical psychologist needs particular skills in:

- two-way communication with clients and colleagues

- working both independently and as part of a team

- analysing each client's situation and therapeutic needs

- therapeutic skills, and an understanding of when a colleague is better able to offer the skills required

- assessing possible ethical issues, for example relating to confidentiality, equality and diversity

- designing research, carrying it out, analysing the findings and writing a report.

More general attributes include being:

- able to empathise with the client, seeing the situation from his or her point of view

- emotionally resilient, so that the client's experiences do not affect your own life

- self-aware, understanding how your own behaviour and attitudes may affect clients

- patient; many clients will only present their case slowly and it can often be a serious error to draw conclusions too soon

- an effective team player, able to influence and motivate others

■ self-motivated, able to work independently, sometimes with difficult and challenging clients

■ intellectually rigorous, so that you can investigate and research issues scientifically and produce valid results.

## The highs and lows

Each clinical psychologist will have very different ideas about what aspects of their work they get most from, and which aspects they find most difficult. The following lists show some possible highs and lows.

Highs include:

■ seeing an improvement in a client's self-belief or ability to function

■ being accepted by the client as someone who is prepared to listen and work with them

■ seeing a client's relief after they have managed to explain some particularly distressing event or aspect of their life

■ working with a varied case load so that no two days are ever the same

■ working in a team of other professionals

■ having the freedom to work independently

■ seeing how the results of your own research can be used to improve the service.

Among the lows are:

■ dealing with the politicking and bureaucracy within the NHS

■ having a heavy workload, which means that not enough time can be spent on each client

■ working with abusive, argumentative or non-appreciative clients

■ conflict with managers, who may not have a psychology or social work background and perhaps cannot understand all of the issues

■ spending excessive time completing paperwork or recording information on computer systems.

# FINDING OUT MORE

You can find out more about work as a clinical psychologist in the following books and websites:

■ Turpin, Graham and Alice Knight (2002) *How to Become a Clinical Psychologist: Getting a Foot in the Door.* Routledge.

■ John Hall and Susan Llewelyn (eds) (2006) *What is Clinical Psychology?* Oxford University Press.

■ The British Psychological Society website, www.bps.org.uk, particularly the Careers and Qualifications section.

■ The www.psyclick.org.uk and www.clinpsy.org.uk websites have been set up by practising clinical psychologists and offer resources for prospective trainees, including information about various courses.

■ The Clearing House for Postgraduate Courses in Clinical Psychology (www.leeds.ac.uk/chpccp/index.html) gives detailed information on specific DClinPsy courses.

# Chapter Four
# EDUCATIONAL PSYCHOLOGY

Educational psychologists work with children or young people who are experiencing problems in school or other educational settings. They aim to ensure effective learning and the healthy emotional development of children and young people from birth to the age of 19 years old.

The primary focus of the work is to help the young person to learn more effectively, but this will often mean working also with social or emotional issues. The key components of an educational psychologist's work can be summarised as consultation, assessment, intervention, training and research.

## WHAT DO EDUCATIONAL PSYCHOLOGISTS DO?

As you can see, the work is varied so will need a variety of skills and knowledge. It involves working with children, parents, teachers and a range of other professionals. It requires interpersonal skills, skills in assessing and analysing situations and people, research skills in analysing data and reporting findings. It also involves knowledge and understanding of a wide range of ages, social and educational situations, and the likely effects of adult interventions in the lives of young people.

## Examples from a case load

To get an idea of the work of an educational psychologist, have a look at some of the brief scenarios below.

■ Peter is an intelligent 13-year-old boy who seriously underachieves at school and is beginning to get in trouble with the police. His school has asked the educational psychologist to assess Peter. The result is a plan for therapy agreed with the school counsellor and a social worker at Peter's local youth club. All three professionals agree to discuss progress in four weeks' time.

■ A number of children at Ryfold School have complained about being bullied by other children. At a meeting at the school the educational psychologist discusses the situation with parents, teachers and school governors. The educational psychologist agrees to develop courses for children in all the affected age groups and to provide ongoing support to those teachers who will give the courses.

■ The educational psychologist and the headteacher of Ryfold School agree a research programme to measure the effectiveness of the courses, to be carried out by the psychologist based on data collected by the school. The long-term aim, if the courses are successful, is to make them available to other schools in the local authority.

■ A recent case of child abuse in the area was heavily publicised in the media. Teachers and social workers are concerned about the welfare of the abused child's sister, Roberta. The educational psychologist has been invited to a case conference at which Roberta's situation will be discussed and the various authorities will develop an action plan for future observation and assessment.

## A typical process

When working with an individual child, the first step is normally an assessment. This will typically involve observing the child in a learning situation, setting tests and analysing the results, and having an initial meeting with the child. Further information can be collected by meeting with the child's teachers, other professionals (such as social workers) and the child's parents or carers.

The educational psychologist may then provide a suitable range of appropriate interventions. These may be learning programmes designed to accelerate learning in specific areas, or to encourage the child to behave in more appropriate ways in the classroom or wider school environment.

It is essential for the educational psychologist to work collaboratively with teachers. After all, the child's teachers have far more contact with the child than any psychologist could do, and it is the teachers who will continue to work with the child in the future.

Educational psychologists also carry out many other tasks. They work directly with young people in groups, for example dealing with issues such as bullying or other forms of anti-social behaviour. They may work with or advise teachers, parents, social workers or other professionals who are involved with an individual child or a group. They may also provide in-service training for teachers and other professionals, for example on topics such as children's behaviour, stress management, or other interpersonal aspects of the school. They may also be asked by educational management to advise on policies and may carry out research, for example on the effectiveness of particular policies on children's performance.

## Typical tasks

To get an idea of the work of an educational psychologist, have a look at how Lancashire Educational Psychology Service describes its work in the box on the following page.

- **'Informal consultation** with teachers about unnamed children or a group of children.

- **Formal consultation** with teachers and parents about a specific child.

- **Telephone consultation** available to parents and schools every afternoon of term time.

- **Assessment** of a specific aspect of a child's development. This assessment may be summative (a summary or snapshot), formative (e.g. to help inform an Individual Educational Plan), diagnostic (to pinpoint very specific strengths or weaknesses) or dynamic (to see how a child makes use of assistance).

- **Intervention and child advocacy work** with some children using Solution Oriented Brief therapy or other techniques.

- **Group work** on social skills or anger management programmes.

- **Whole school work** regarding in-service training for teachers, policy development work or critical incident support work.

- **Children's Services Authority work** including assessment of children out of school or placed in independent schools, the provision of psychological advice as part of a statutory assessment, representation at SEN tribunals, contribution to policy development, and research and development.

- **The development of new techniques** or materials including ways of assessment and approaches to intervention.

- **Work with other agencies** including Child and Adolescent Mental Health Services, the local school effectiveness service, and community paediatricians.'

(Source: Educational Psychology Service, www.lancashire.gov.uk)

## Work settings

Most educational psychologists in England, Scotland and Wales are employed by local authorities. In Northern Ireland the employers are generally the various education and library boards. Individuals or teams of educational psychologists may work in schools, colleges, nurseries and special units.

Other public sector posts are available in social service assessment centres, hospital-based paediatric assessment units and child psychiatric units. You could also be employed in a research establishment or in a university.

Educational psychologists also work, often on a consultancy or freelance basis, for charities, in training organisations, in independent schools or with families.

## Studying on a DEdPsy

Study for a Doctorate in Child Psychology is largely based on research and individual study. However, it is important to realise that educational psychologists need to consider the development of the child from a number of theoretical perspectives.

For example, the King's College London course information comments, 'The programme embraces a social constructivist approach and is based on an interactionist psychological perspective.' In other words, your study would be based on an approach that emphasises the importance of social settings in which groups construct knowledge for one another. It focuses on an individual's learning that takes place because of their interactions in a group.

The Newcastle University course contains five modules: two in advanced current issues in educational psychology, and three in research methodology appropriate to educational psychology practice (see www. ncl.ac.uk).

The Cardiff University prospectus on its website describes the 2009 course as follows:

> *The curriculum covers six themes:*
>
> - *Research methods in educational psychology*
> - *Processes and methods of assessment*

- *The psychology of learning: managing change*
- *The psychology of behaviour: managing change*
- *Understanding and working with groups, systems and organisations: managing change*
- *The role of the educational psychologist.'*

(From the description of the DEdPsy course at Cardiff University, http://courses.cf.ac.uk)

Considering all of the above points, it's clear that to study for a DEdPsy you will need to start with a good theoretical grounding in the psychology of child development and of research methods. The course will then enable you to use and further develop your knowledge in both areas.

If you don't feel confident in your knowledge at this stage, then remember that there are master's level courses that can raise your levels of skills and understanding.

## ENTRY REQUIREMENTS

All educational psychologists in England, Wales and Northern Ireland need to have a Doctorate in Educational Psychology (DEdPsy) from an accredited course.

To be accepted for a three-year doctorate course, you will generally need at least a 2:1 degree in a relevant subject, be able to show that you have research skills, and show that you have carried out relevant work experience.

If you have a 2:2 you will normally need to take a relevant master's course before you can be considered for a DEdPsy course. The master's should generally relate to education and preferably involve relevant practical experience. You may be accepted for a DEdPsy course with a 2:2 if you have extensive relevant experience in education.

You also need the Graduate Basis for Registration (GBR) of the British Psychological Society (BPS). Only certain accredited psychology degrees will make you eligible for GBR; others may only make you eligible for Graduate Membership of the BPS. Graduate Membership does not make you eligible for a DEdPsy course and you will need to take a conversion course or a qualifying examination. To find out which degree courses are accredited, and for more on conversion courses and qualifying examinations, see Chapter 9 or the careers section of the British Psychological Society website (www.bps.org.uk).

The entry requirements and training in Scotland are rather different and a Scottish educational psychologist may gain an Award in Educational Psychology on the basis of a two-year master's in educational psychology and successfully completing a one-year probation and supervised practice. Acceptance for a master's course requires GBR status and at least two years' experience of working with children or young people. Some Scottish local authorities employ trainee educational psychologists and this can be a useful way of gaining relevant experience before taking the MSc (EdPsy). For more information on working in Scotland, search for Educational Psychology (Scotland) on the British Psychological Society website (www.bps.org.uk).

## Studying psychology at university and school

If you are currently studying at school or college and think you may later wish to become an educational psychologist, it's worth thinking in advance about how you could most easily progress towards that profession.

Studying psychology at GCSE or A-level will give you a good idea of the basics of the subject. It is also a useful preparation for almost any degree, particularly in subjects such as medicine, the sciences and social sciences. A-level psychology is not a requirement if you want to study the subject at university, though it will be useful. Whatever subjects you choose, however, do remember that you may need to show at least some understanding of the use of scientific methods.

When selecting a psychology course at university, it may be useful to take a joint-honours course that combines psychology with a major school subject such as maths or English. However, remember that not all courses will give you Graduate Basis for Registration (GBR) of the British Psychological Society (BPS). If you think you may want to work as an educational psychologist in the future, it is important to apply only for accredited courses.

## Mature students

Since acceptance for training as an educational psychologist places such an emphasis on previous experience, it is quite common for mature students to study on DEdPsy courses. Thinking of what educational psychology involves, you will also realise that some degree of maturity and self-knowledge is needed if you are to work with emotionally disturbed children and their families, and if you are to work effectively to influence other professionals.

If you are thinking of applying as a mature student but are unsure about whether your experience and qualifications are suitable, it will be worthwhile contacting the relevant university to find out whether or not particular experience in, say, education, social or community work is relevant.

## What non-academic skills do I need?

Apart from academic qualifications, you will need to be an excellent communicator with sensitivity, tact and diplomacy, coupled with the ability to be assertive, persuasive and an effective facilitator. You must also possess strong negotiating, administration and time-management skills.

## Work experience

To be accepted on to a DEdPsy course you must demonstrate that you have relevant experience of working with children in education, childcare or in community work. You will generally need to show that you have at least a year's experience of this type.

Experience as a teacher (and the knowledge gained on an education course) is very relevant and may give you exemption from parts of the doctorate course.

Some local education authorities employ assistant educational psychologists. This is a useful way of getting practical experience, gaining an understanding of the work and developing relevant skills.

On a DEdPsy course the second and third years generally involve gaining practical experience by working for a local education authority as a trainee educational psychologist.

## International applicants

Only EU applicants can be considered for entry onto DEdPsy courses. However, nationals of other EU countries should remember that the DEdPsy is based on working in the UK education system.

People from non-EU countries would need to apply for a work permit, and cannot guarantee that they will be allowed to work in the UK for long periods. As a result they cannot usually be considered for DEdPsy courses.

## What are my chances?

There are about four times as many applicants as places on DEdPsy courses, but once trained there are jobs available and there is currently (2009) an overall shortage.

For more information on suitable courses and entry procedures, search for educational psychology professional entry training providers on the website of the Children's Workforce Development Council (www. cwdcouncil.org.uk).

Note that the CWDC deals only with English universities. For courses elsewhere, search for information on educational psychology on the following websites. Wales: www.cardiff.ac.uk; Northern Ireland: www.psych.qub.ac.uk; and Scotland: www.dundee.ac.uk or www. strath.ac.uk.

## Describing your relevant experience and knowledge

When applying for a DEdPsy you will generally have to present a short (perhaps two-page) summary explaining why you think that you are ready to follow the course. The descriptions in the box opposite summarise the University College London guidance on writing this part of the application. The description should give you some idea of the level of experience and knowledge that you will need if you are to have a reasonable chance of success in such an application.

1 Knowledge you have gained of the organisation and operation of schools and pre-school provision and of the most important current issues within children's services.

2 Knowledge of psychological theory and research on children's development and learning and the ability to apply it to practice contexts, focusing on one or two clear and reflective examples.

3 Knowledge about the work of educational psychologists and evidence of commitment to the profession. You need to show that you have detailed knowledge about the range of work educational psychologists do, obtained from a variety of credible sources and that your commitment to the profession is sufficiently strong that you can be relied upon to invest the effort needed to complete a challenging and intensive three-year training programme.

4 Ability to identify skills/knowledge especially relevant to training as an educational psychologist and explain their relevance.

5 Clear and coherent written communication skills. This will be judged from your personal statement.

(Based on *Application and selection* on www.ucl.ac.uk)

**As a sixth form student Jane worked in her holidays for voluntary organisations that provided holidays for disadvantaged children.**

She wondered about going into social work but was unsure whether she had the inner strength to deal with difficult problems all day and every day.

Jane eventually decided to study biology at Exeter University and gained a 2:1. 'I wondered then whether I wanted to study the subject more deeply, perhaps doing a master's or doctorate, but decided to go into secondary school teaching. I thought that I could combine my interest in history with my enthusiasm for working with young people.'

During her last year as an undergraduate, Jane was accepted for a Certificate in Education course. After the course, she did her probationary year working in a rural secondary school. She stayed in that school for four years, becoming increasingly interested in the pastoral side of school life. She became a deputy head of year and then applied for a head of year post in a school in the local large town. She worked as head of year for five years, taking a number of Open University courses in child psychology and related subjects.

During her annual appraisal meeting with her headteacher, Jane realised that she was becoming more interested in working with individual children than she was in working in the classroom. She decided to try to become a child psychologist and contacted her local university department to find out what qualifications she would need. To her pleasant surprise she discovered that two more OU courses and the study for her Certificate in Education, combined with her extensive practical experience, would be sufficient to qualify her for a DEdPsy course.

Jane qualified as a chartered educational psychologist 10 years ago. She has worked in the south-west of England for all of that time and comments, 'I suppose I could try for promotion, but to be honest it would probably mean less contact with individual children and more meetings. I think I'll stay where I am at least until the children leave home.'

# IS THIS THE CAREER FOR ME?

## The practicalities

The working hours are mainly nine to five, but some evening and weekend work may be involved, for example to allow for meetings with working parents.

Most positions exist in large towns and cities. Those who work in rural areas must expect to spend considerable time travelling to meet children, teachers, colleagues and parents, or to attend meetings.

The work can be stressful, since it often involves contact with disturbed or distressed children and young people, and their parents. Educational psychologists also come up against the practical situations in which there is insufficient funding to completely satisfy the needs of a particular child or group of children.

Part-time working is possible and may allow other self-employment or freelance work. For example, a local authority psychologist may also set up a private practice, or work in a local private school.

## Career prospects

Typical salary ranges are currently (2009):

- trainee educational psychologist: £21,000 to £29,000

- chartered educational psychologist £31,000 to £41,000

- senior educational psychologist £41,000 to £56,000.

At present the career prospects for educational psychologists are very good, with a number of vacancies. It's also likely that there will be long-term growth in the provision of psychological and social support for children and young people.

## Career progression

Small local authority educational psychology departments are typically headed by a senior or principal educational psychologist, with a team of chartered and trainee educational psychologists. In other words, there are generally only three steps in the career ladder. However, large authorities may organise psychological services on the basis of districts or perhaps specialist units, and so may offer more-senior posts.

Educational psychologists also have the option of moving into specialist areas, or moving from a local authority to work with large organisations in areas such as managing people with disabilities, or working in training departments. There may also be scope for consultancy work with special schools, private schools or other education organisations.

## Self-assessment

In the following sections are brief descriptions of what the job is like in practice, what particular skills and attributes you'll need, and what educational psychologists find particularly good (and bad) about their work. The comments have deliberately been kept brief so that you can use them as a checklist and assess whether you would suit this career, and whether it would suit you.

## The work in practice

The main tasks are:

- working with a wide range of children, parents and teachers

- assessing young people's learning and emotional needs and diagnosing the problems being experienced by children, teachers, schools and parents

- working as part of a multi-disciplinary team to support individual children

- working to develop training and encourage more effective ways of working with particular children or groups of children

- writing reports to make formal recommendations on action to be taken, including formal statements

- liaising with other professionals and facilitating meetings, discussions and courses

- developing and reviewing policies

- carrying out research, generally into the effectiveness of particular educational methods or systems.

## Skills and attributes

The effective educational psychologist needs particular skills in:

- two-way communication with children, parents, teachers and colleagues

- analysing each child's situation and therapeutic needs

- working both independently and as part of a team

- advising, negotiating, persuading and supporting teachers, parents and other education professionals

- assessing possible ethical issues, for example relating to confidentiality, equality and diversity

- designing research, carrying it out, analysing the findings and writing a report.

More general attributes include:

- very good interpersonal skills that enable effective work with children, young adults, parents, teachers and other professionals

- ability to empathise with the child, parents and teachers, seeing the situation from their various points of view

- emotionally resilient, so that the child's, parents' and teachers' experiences do not affect your own life

- ability to stand back from an emotional response to the child and rigorously evaluate the possible courses of future action

- self-awareness, understanding how your own behaviour and attitudes may affect clients

■ patience; many children will only explain their situation slowly and it can often be a serious error to draw conclusions too soon

■ being an effective team player, able to influence and motivate others

■ self-motivation, able to work independently, sometimes with difficult and challenging clients

■ intellectually rigorous, so that you can investigate and research issues scientifically and produce valid results.

## The highs and lows

Each educational psychologist will have very different ideas about what aspects of their work they get most from, and which aspects they find most difficult. The following lists show some possible highs and lows.

Highs include:

■ seeing an improvement in a child's, or a teacher's, self-belief or ability to function

■ being accepted by a 'difficult' child as someone who is prepared to listen and work with them

■ working with a varied range of parents and professionals

■ having a varied case load so that no two days are ever the same

■ having the freedom to work independently

■ seeing training that you have developed being used effectively in a school

■ seeing how the results of your own research can be used to improve the service.

Among the lows are:

■ working with abusive, argumentative or non-appreciative parents

■ conflict with teachers, who may be unaware of the limitations on the support that educational psychologists can give

- having a case load that is overloaded with assessments, giving little time to plan interventions and programmes

- dealing with the bureaucracy within the education system

- spending excessive time completing paperwork or recording information on computer systems.

# FINDING OUT MORE

You can find out more about work as an educational psychologist in the following journal and websites:

- the journal *Educational Psychology in Practice* http://www.tandf. co.uk/journals/carfax/02667363.html

- the British Psychological Society website, www.bps.org.uk, particularly the Careers and Qualifications section

- the Association of Educational Psychologists, at www.aep.org.uk

- the Children's Workforce Development Council (which acts as the clearing house for educational psychology courses in England), at www.cwdcouncil.org.uk

- the *Award in Ed Psychol (Scot) Handbook* for information about requirements in Scotland, available on the British Psychological Society website, www.bps.org.uk.

# Chapter Five
# NEUROPSYCHOLOGY

Neuropsychology is the scientific study of the relationships between the brain and behaviour. Clinical neuropsychologists almost always enter the profession after training and experience as a clinical psychologist (see Chapter 3), or as an educational psychologist if they want to work with children and young people in paediatric neuropsychology (see Chapter 4).

Neuropsychologists generally work in the health service, often working in partnership with other health professionals and social workers. They work with clients who have psychological problems or other difficulties linked to brain injury or disease. Neuropsychologists work with people of all ages who may have, for example, suffered brain injury, stroke, toxic and metabolic disorders, tumours and neurodegenerative diseases such as Alzheimer's.

As a clinical neuropsychologist you would generally work through a three-stage process, starting with assessing the client. You would then diagnose the problem and devise a treatment plan, perhaps involving drugs and working with carers.

Academic neuropsychologists may work for the NHS or for universities and carry out research, for example studying the brain functions of healthy human beings or monitoring the effects of pharmaceutical drugs.

All neuropsychologists may also work as expert witnesses in court cases, for example assessing the degree of damage caused by a road accident.

If you think neuropsychology might be for you, this chapter describes the work in some detail and then explains what qualifications and training you will need. It ends with a summary of what the work involves, of the 'highs' and 'lows' that you might expect, and checklists that you can use to assess whether you have the relevant attributes and skills.

# WHAT DO NEUROPSYCHOLOGISTS DO?

## Examples from a case load

To get an idea of the work of a neuropsychologist, have a look at some of the very brief scenarios below.

■ Michael has been referred to a hospital neuropsychologist by his GP. He appears to be suffering from the early stages of Alzheimer's disease. The neuropsychologist carries out an assessment and confirms the GP's fears. The neuropsychologist then has to explain the likely development of the disease to Michael and his wife, consider whether pharmaceutical drugs should be given, and inform the relevant other professionals, who will then plan further support that Michael and his wife will need in the future.

■ Nazeem is 21 and has recently been knocked over by a car and suffered head injuries. His neuropsychologist predicts that Nazeem will need full-time care for the rest of his life and is currently working with the family and relevant health and care professionals to plan how this may be arranged. It is likely that a future court case will be needed to decide whether Nazeem's family can claim the costs of providing that care from the car driver's insurance company. The neuropsychologist keeps careful records of all diagnoses and actions so that they can be presented in the court case.

■ Olwen is 40 and very fit. However, she has suffered a number of 'blackouts' recently. The neuropsychologist decides to carry out a brain scan to see if the cause could be damage to a particular part of the brain.

■  Working as a research neuropsychologist, Dr Parry contacts a number of neuropsychologists working in hospitals throughout the UK. She asks for data about people who may have a type of anomia in which they forget words once they try to say them aloud. She hopes that she can identify why this may happen, and eventually hopes to find a way of identifying the problem in the early stages and preventing its further development.

Those four cases are all typical of situations in a neuropsychologist's work. As you can see, they're pretty varied so will need a range of skills and knowledge. Just as importantly, they will need good interpersonal skills: think how difficult it would be to tell Michael or Nazeem's family what their future holds.

Clinical neuropsychologists need to be able to work not only on the neuropsychology elements of their role; they also need to be able to plan behavioural and therapeutic programmes for the client; and they must work with the client's family and carers, and with a range of other professionals.

## Neuropsychology in more detail

Neuropsychologists need a theoretical knowledge of the anatomy of the brain (neuroanatomy) and the problems that can occur within the brain (neuropathology). They use a range of assessment methods to understand, prevent and relieve physically based dysfunction of the brain which is causing physical or psychological problems.

Note that neuropsychology differs from neurosurgery and neurology. Both of those studies are medically based. A neurosurgeon is a physician who may carry out surgery on the nervous system or the spine. A neurologist is a physician who works with disorders of the nervous system, generally (but not always), focusing on medical treatments rather than psychological ones.

Clinical neuropsychologists most commonly work in one or more of the following settings:

■  **Acute settings.** Neuropsychologists may work in a regional neurosciences centre, working with neurosurgeons, neurologists and others. Wherever possible, they work with early effects of trauma and neurological disease. They may then refer patients to rehabilitation centres for longer-term work.

- **Rehabilitation centres.** These provide longer-term assessment, training and support for people who have sustained brain injury or have other neurological problems. The neuropsychologist will work in a multi-disciplinary team that aims to help the patients recover, minimise their disabilities, and prepare them for returning home or to a residential centre.

- **Community services.** Neuropsychologists may also work with those who have returned home or who live in residential centres.

- **Expert witness work.** Experienced neuropsychologists may also act, often in addition to their normal work, as expert witnesses for the courts.

## Neuropsychological assessments

Neuropsychological assessment generally begins with assessment of a person's cognitive skills, usually after some sort of brain injury or some disease is suspected. This may be based on working with the patient; for example, testing reasoning and problem-solving skills, learning and recall processes, testing concentration or perception, language processes, or the ability to control movement. One website listing the 'commonly used' tests contained 70 such tests, from the 'Ammons Quick Test' (one type of intelligence test) to the 'Word Memory Test'. See www.brainsource.com/nptests.htm for the complete list.

The neuropsychologist will at all times also be aware that the problem may be caused by, for example, a problem with blood flow in the brain, chronically poor nutrition, or with damage caused by drug use.

Overall, the neuropsychologist will try to collect and analyse information collected from the client's psychosocial history, personality, medical and physical health history. Using that analysis, the aim is to understand the client's situation and plan treatment and potential rehabilitation.

The neuropsychologist will typically follow a three-stage process of assessment, diagnosis, and then working with the client and various other professionals. Thinking again of the case examples listed at the start of the chapter, the neuropsychologist needs to decide whether pharmaceutical drugs will help Alzheimer's patient Michael at this stage. There is also the task of planning the increasing levels of support that will be needed as the illness progresses. Olwen's situation is more complex. Her problem may be caused by a number of factors, for example blood flow in the brain, migraines or diabetes. The action to be taken and the long-term consequences are very different in each case and the neuropsychologist will need to carry out a careful assessment before making any decisions.

## Work settings

Clinical neuropsychologists work mainly in hospitals and psychiatric units. They almost always work as part of a team including neurosurgeons, neurologists and other health professionals, with close links to a range of support workers and other social workers. In rehabilitation centres the neuropsychologist will often be the leader of a multi-disciplinary team.

Other neuropsychologists work in laboratories to study the brain functions of healthy human beings or to monitor the effects of experimental pharmaceutical drugs.

Those neuropsychologists who work in the National Health Service can follow a clearly defined career structure. They may also choose to combine NHS work with research work, teaching or training.

## Research

Clinical neuropsychologists are also expected to carry out their own research, generally into the effectiveness of a particular treatment or other aspects of the help provided for clients. Most psychologists will carry out this research independently, so need to have a good theoretical background and experience in designing and implementing research projects.

Research of various types is an important part of every Doctorate in Neuropsychology course, and trainees are expected to have a good grounding in research methods, in addition to their understanding of clinical or education psychology, if they are to be accepted onto such a course.

Other neuropsychologists carry out research full-time, for example working for universities, research establishments or pharmaceutical organisations.

# ENTRY REQUIREMENTS

## Clinical neuropsychologist

If you want to become a clinical neuropsychologist, you will need first to qualify as a clinical psychologist or educational psychologist. This involves three steps.

1   Taking an accredited psychology degree or a conversion course or the qualifying exam.

2   Following an accredited postgraduate training programme.

3   Registering as a chartered clinical or educational psychologist.

You will then need to carry out further study and work experience linked to a supervised study programme in neuropsychology, involving elements of knowledge, research and practice. The knowledge component will be assessed by written examination, the research element by presenting a research paper, and the practice element by showing case studies and a log of experience gained. You can find further information on this by searching for the Practitioner Full Membership Qualification in Neuropsychology on the British Psychological Society website (www. bps.org.uk).

The knowledge and research elements of this process may be studied independently or through a university department. For example, Cardiff University offers 'an MSc in Clinical Neuropsychology for post-doctoral clinical psychologists, which provides the underpinning knowledge and research components of the Practitioner Full Membership Qualification (PFMQ) awarded by the BPS Division of Neuropsychology (D.o.N)' (http://medicine.moodle.gla.ac.uk).

## Research neuropsychologist

To work towards becoming a research neuropsychologist, you can follow a master's or doctorate research-based course in neuropsychology, or a specialist branch of the subject. This will deepen your understanding of the theory of neuropsychology and also of the theory and practice of research.

## Studying psychology at university and school

If you are currently studying at school or college and think you may later wish to become a neuropsychologist, it's worth thinking in advance how you could most easily progress towards that profession.

Studying psychology at GCSE or A-level will give you a good idea of the basics of the subject. It is also a useful preparation for almost any degree, particularly in subjects such as medicine, the sciences and social sciences. A-level psychology is not a requirement if you want to study the subject at university, though it will be useful. Whatever subjects you choose, however, do remember that you may need to show at least some understanding of the use of scientific methods.

When selecting a psychology course at university, remember that not all of them will give you Graduate Basis for Registration (GBR) of the British Psychological Society (BPS). If you think you may want to work as a neuropsychologist in the future, it is important to apply only for accredited courses.

## Mature students

Since acceptance for training as a neuropsychologist places such an emphasis on previous experience and training, only experienced practitioners train for careers in clinical neuropsychology.

In contrast, careers in research in neuropsychology are suitable for people of any age who have obtained a relevant postgraduate research-based qualification.

If you are thinking of applying as a mature student but are unsure about whether your experience and qualifications are suitable, it will be worthwhile discussing your plans with someone who has experience and knowledge of the British Psychological Society system.

## Professional descriptions

At the time of writing (2009) changes are being considered in relation to the status of neuropsychologists within the British Psychological Society. Their website explains that members should not use a title such as 'Chartered Clinical Neuropsychologist', but should instead be called 'Clinical Neuropsychologist' or 'Consultant Clinical Neuropsychologist'.

However, the BPS also comment that this situation is likely to change, and that further guidance will become available from the Society when the changes have been made (see the Division of Neuropsychology section of the www.bps.org.uk website).

To become an accredited clinical neuropsychologist, you would need to first have chartered status as a clinical psychologist or education psychologist.

## International applicants

Neuropsychology courses designed for research careers are suitable for people from the UK, EU and other countries.

However, preparation for a clinical neuropsychology career involves showing proof of work experience, normally within the NHS. As a result, this is not suitable for people from countries outside Europe, who would need to apply for a work permit and cannot guarantee that they will be allowed to work in the UK for long periods.

**Brenda is a neuropsychologist working in a rehabilitation centre in a large city.**

'It took me a while to decide that neuropsychology was my main interest. I'd always been interested in people and started off studying sociology at university. The trouble was that seemed to be about people in general, and I decided I was more interested in individuals, so I transferred to the psychology course.

'I qualified with first-class honours but was very unsure what I wanted to do next, so took a year out and went travelling. Two years later I was in Australia, needed some money, so got a job as a cleaner in a centre that worked to rehabilitate people suffering from severe drug and alcohol problems. It was really impressive to see the range of approaches that the centre used, and the care that everyone seemed to show.

'Returning to the UK I decided that I wanted to work in a similar centre, but in a way that used my knowledge of psychology. My plan was to become a neuropsychologist. Unfortunately, looking it up I found that I would need to train first to become a clinical psychologist.

'Based on my degree, and the work experience I'd gained when travelling and during my first degree, I was accepted for a doctorate course. Three years later I qualified and found a job working in a hospital with a very experienced senior clinical psychologist. He was great, and helped me to plan how I could most easily move eventually into neuropsychology. On the other hand, he also made sure that I also focused on my work in clinical psychology.

'After five years in the hospital we both felt that I had sufficient experience and I started looking for a supervisor. In the end I decided to carry out my study for the BPS's Practitioner Full Membership Qualification through my local university. This meant I could easily meet my supervisor and had a chance to talk to other students. Because of my work commitments it took me a little while to complete the research work, but I eventually qualified three years ago.

'Six months later I moved to new work in a centre for elderly people: some have had strokes, others have neurodegenerative diseases. It's a whole range of problems like that. Many of them won't recover fully, so a lot of the job is about helping people to work with the distress and then practical questions about how to live as comfortably as possible. There's also quite a lot of contact with husbands, wives or other carers, and also with the various social workers and care workers. It's odd: you'd think it would be really miserable work, but there's actually a lot of laughter around. You certainly feel as though you're doing something useful.'

# IS THIS THE CAREER FOR ME?

## The practicalities

Work as a clinical neuropsychologist can be stressful, since it often involves contact with people who are disabled or distressed in some way. Many aspects of neuropsychology also relate to people with problems that involve long-term decline or are terminal.

The working hours are mainly nine to five, but some evening and weekend work may be involved. It may be necessary to be available on call in case of emergencies.

Most positions exist in large towns and cities, with fewer opportunities in rural areas. The neuropsychologist will sometimes have to travel locally to attend meetings or meet colleagues.

Positions with the NHS may allow other self-employment or freelance work. For example, a neuropsychologist may set up a private clinical practice, or get work assessing accident victims for the courts.

Work as a research neuropsychologist will almost always be from nine to five, based in a laboratory or research establishment. Most positions exist in large towns and cities and travel is rarely required.

## Career prospects

Pay in the NHS is on the same scales as that of clinical psychologists. Qualified neuropsychologists are paid on scale 7, a scale that currently

(2009) runs from about £29,000 to £38,000. Senior, experienced neuropsychologists with responsibilities for departments or large specialist sections may earn in the range £44,000 to £80,000.

Many senior neuropsychologists can also substantially add to their income by undertaking private consultancy as expert witnesses in personal injury cases.

Research neuropsychologists typically earn in the range £18,000 to £24,000 initially, though a research fellow may earn up to £35,000.

At present the career prospects for clinical and research neuropsychologists are very good, with a number of vacancies. It's also likely that there will be long-term growth in the provision of psychological and social support, particularly for the increasing proportion of elderly people in the UK population.

## Self-assessment

In the following sections are brief descriptions of what the job is like in practice, what particular skills and attributes you'll need, and what psychologists find particularly good (and bad) about their work. The comments have deliberately been kept brief so that you can use them as a checklist and assess whether you would suit this career, and whether it would suit you.

## The work in practice

The main tasks for the clinical neuropsychologist are:

- working with a wide range of people who are disabled, distressed or dysfunctional, and may have problems that involve long-term decline or are terminal

- working as part of a multi-disciplinary team typically including neurosurgeons, neurologists, psychotherapists, and care and social workers

- using a range of assessment methods to diagnose the problems being experienced by a range of clients

- selecting and planning a suitable programme of treatment or care for each client, often involving work with other professionals

- carrying out therapeutic work with clients, where there is a match between the client's needs and the neuropsychologist's skills and experience

- carrying out research, generally into the effectiveness of particular therapeutic methods or systems.

## Skills and attributes

The effective clinical neuropsychologist needs particular skills in:

- two-way communication with clients and colleagues

- working both independently and as part of a team

- analysing each client's situation and therapeutic or care needs

- therapeutic skills, and an understanding of when a colleague is better able to offer the skills required

- assessing possible ethical issues, for example relating to levels of treatment, terminal illness, confidentiality, equality and diversity

- designing research, carrying it out, analysing the findings and writing a report.

More general attributes include being:

- able to empathise with the client, carers and co-workers, seeing the situation from their points of view

- knowledgeable about the wide range of possible causes of neurological problems

- emotionally resilient, so that the clients' experiences do not affect your own life

- self-aware, understanding how your own behaviour and attitudes may affect clients

- an effective team player, able to influence and motivate others

- intellectually rigorous, so that you can investigate and research issues scientifically and produce valid results.

## The highs and lows

Each clinical neuropsychologist will have very different ideas about what aspects of their work they get most from, and which aspects they find most difficult. The following lists show some possible highs and lows.

Highs include:

- seeing an improvement in a client's health or ability to function

- being accepted by the client as someone who is prepared to listen and work with them

- working with a varied case load so that no two days are ever the same

- working in a team of other professionals

- working with dedicated carers

- seeing how the results of your own research can be used to improve the service.

Among the lows are:

- dealing with the politicking and bureaucracy within the NHS

- having a heavy workload, which means that not enough time can be spent on each client

- working with abusive, argumentative or non-appreciative clients

- having to explain the likely results of terminal illness or the stages of long-term decline

- conflict with managers, who may not have a psychology or medical background and perhaps cannot understand all of the issues

- spending excessive time completing paperwork or recording information on computer systems.

# FINDING OUT MORE

You can find out more about work as a clinical neuropsychologist in the following books and websites.

- For a description of the approaches used by clinical neuropsychologists, see L.H. Goldstein and J.E. McNeil (eds) (2003) *Clinical Neuropsychology: A Practical Guide to Assessment and Management for Clinicians.* WileyBlackwell.

- The British Psychological Society website www.bps.org.uk, particularly the links to neuropsychology in the Careers and Qualifications section.

# Chapter Six
# FORENSIC PSYCHOLOGY

Forensic psychologists work with psychological aspects of the law, working with the police, the prison system, or in university or government research. For example, they may apply psychological theories to criminal investigations, criminal behaviour and the treatment of criminals. In the media you may see forensic psychologists referred to as profilers, criminal psychologists or criminologists.

If you think forensic psychology might be for you, this chapter describes the work in some detail and then explains what qualifications and training you will need. It ends with a summary of what the work involves, of the 'highs' and 'lows' that you might expect, and checklists that you can use to assess whether you have the relevant attributes and skills.

## WHAT DO FORENSIC PSYCHOLOGISTS DO?

The six examples from a case load described below are all typical of situations in forensic psychologists' work. They're pretty varied so will need a range of skills and knowledge; and no one forensic psychologist would carry out all of those tasks. Just as importantly, they will need good interpersonal skills and confidence in their own abilities: think how difficult it might be to work with a victim and offender (as Ken does), or with a potentially violent criminal like Gary.

## Examples from a case load

To get an idea of the work of a forensic psychologist, have a look at some of the very brief scenarios below.

- The police have been investigating a series of murders in a small city. They note that there are similarities between the murders and ask a forensic psychologist to identify possible characteristics that the murderer may have.

- Gary has been arrested and is to be tried for a series of violent attacks. He has a history of mental illness and the court asks the forensic psychologist to advise on whether to send him to prison or hospital.

- Hannah works as a chartered forensic psychologist. She receives a phone call late one night in which the local police ask her to attend a house where a man has taken his ex-wife hostage.

- Indira is the senior forensic psychologist in a large prison. She chairs a meeting at which the prison's psychologists, therapists and senior prison officers plan changes to the programme for giving support to psychologists, social workers and health workers in training.

- Jack is a forensic psychologist in training, working in a prison. He currently works with eight individual prisoners, focusing on his specialities of stress management and anger management.

- Ken works for the probation service and is currently developing a scheme during which young offenders meet with their victims as part of their rehabilitation programme.

Forensic psychologists need to be able not only to understand the psychological factors that may affect their clients. They also need to be able to plan behavioural and therapeutic programmes for the client; they may need to work with victims; and will have to work with a range of other professionals.

## The forensic psychologist's focus

Before reading more, it's important to focus on the approach that the forensic psychologist will take when working with clients. The key is the word 'client'. Where others in the legal system may focus on 'offenders', forensic psychologists try to adopt a non-discriminatory and non-judgemental approach. The aim is to empower the clients, building a relationship with them to maximise the chance of successful rehabilitation.

## Forensic psychology in more detail

Forensic psychologists most commonly get asked to work on four fundamental tasks. The first is to apply psychological theories to criminal investigations. What guidance may an understanding of criminal behaviour give that will help the police to catch criminals and prevent further crimes? What information can the psychologist give that will help the court to make a rational decision in a particular case? Television police programmes may suggest that using psychology in investigations is a matter of waiting for an inspirational thought, but in practice it's more likely to involve crime analysis and prisoner profiling techniques based on statistical analysis.

The second major task is to understand psychological problems associated with criminal behaviour. This may be used to plan future treatment, for example advising the courts on whether probation, prison or hospital may be most suitable. It may also be used when advising parole boards and mental health tribunals, for example when advising whether a prisoner is ready to be released, and when answering questions about any future risks to society.

The third major task is to plan suitable treatment and rehabilitation programmes for the offender while in prison or on probation. For example, what may be the best way of modifying the offender's past behaviour; what advice can the psychologist give to the staff who work with that particular prisoner; and what can be done to minimise the stress experienced by prisoners and the staff who work with them? Typical rehabilitation programmes include anger management, stress management, social skills training, wider education programmes, and treatment for drug or alcohol addiction. Typical support for staff might include courses on stress management, coping with bullying, and techniques for hostage negotiation.

Finally, like most psychologists, forensic psychologists carry out research. They will often be asked to provide research-based evidence to support their practice: for example, did a particular new therapeutic programme actually reduce re-offending rates when prisoners were released?

## Assessment

One-to-one assessments form a major part of the work of forensic psychologists based in prisons or hospitals, and also of those psychologists who are asked to advise the courts.

The courts will be interested in, for example, whether offenders have the mental capacity to understand the legal actions being taken by the court, or whether they can be considered responsible for their actions at the time of the crime.

Assessment of prisoners will typically occur when they first arrive at the prison and at regular intervals after that. Assessment may also be carried out to assess the risk of re-offending, for example if a long-term prisoner or a sex offender is being released into the community. Thirdly, the psychologist may be asked to assess the risk of suicide or self-injury.

The range of tests available is similar to that available during neuropsychological assessment (see Chapter 5); for example, to assess a person's cognitive skills, or to identify brain injury or disease, or damage caused by drugs or alcohol. This generally involves testing reasoning and problem-solving skills, learning and recall processes, testing concentration or perception, language processes, or the ability to control movement. One website listing the 'commonly used' tests contained 70 such tests, from the 'Ammons Quick Test' (one type of intelligence test) to the 'Word Memory Test'. See www.brainsource.com/nptests.htm for the complete list.

## Communicating the results of the assessment

The forensic psychologist will frequently need to present the findings of the assessment to other professionals, the courts and the client.

Before selecting this career, you need to assess whether you could communicate effectively in all of those situations. For example, would you be able to explain a prisoner's condition to other psychologists, social workers and prison officers in a way that clearly explained how it may affect each of them? Would you be able to justify your findings when cross-examined by a barrister? And could you explain to a sex offender why you had decided that he could not be allowed to leave the prison?

As a forensic psychologist you would also need to communicate effectively in meetings and conferences, and work with hospital staff, prison officers, the police, social workers, probation officers, lawyers and judges.

## Treatment

The methods used in the therapeutic treatment of prisoners or offenders on probation will vary widely. When dealing with specific types of criminal behaviour it may be possible to use carefully focused short-term cognitive-behavioural group programmes. For more deep-seated issues, longer-term therapy may be needed. As a forensic psychologist you need to carefully assess which therapy is most suitable, and also decide whether you are qualified to give that treatment or should refer the client to another, better qualified, therapist.

## Work settings

Forensic psychologists are most commonly employed by the Prison Service. Note that this service employs people in prisons and also in the Home Office Research and Development Unit.

You could also find forensic psychologists in rehabilitation units and secure hospitals (employed by the NHS), in the police service, in young offenders' units and the probation service, or in private consultancy.

## Security

Working in prisons and special hospitals means that you will need to be particularly aware of security issues. For example, you may be searched each day on arrival and when leaving, and perhaps while you move between areas of your workplace. You are likely to be observed by closed-circuit television systems for much of your time. You may need to be escorted at times, perhaps by officers whose working style differs significantly from your own.

## Research

Forensic psychologists are also expected to carry out their own research, generally into criminal behaviour or the effectiveness of a particular therapeutic treatment or rehabilitation programme. Most psychologists will carry out this research independently so need to have a good theoretical background and experience in designing and implementing research projects.

Research of various types is an important part of every postgraduate course in forensic psychology, and trainees are expected to have a good grounding in research methods if they are to be accepted onto such a course. During such a course you are likely to study the psychology of criminal behaviour, and social psychology of the law and the treatment of offenders.

Other forensic psychologists carry out research full-time, for example working for universities or the Home Office Research and Development Unit.

# ENTRY REQUIREMENTS

Provided you have a degree from a suitable psychology course, there are two stages to becoming a chartered forensic psychologist.

The first stage is to take an accredited master's course in forensic psychology. You can find suitable courses on the BPS website (www. bps.org.uk). Most universities require at least a 2:1 degree, though some will accept a 2:2.

The second stage involves two years of supervised practice in the workplace. Completing the two stages successfully will qualify you for the British Psychological Society's Diploma in Forensic Psychology.

You need to check that your first degree gives you Graduate Basis for Registration (GBR) of the British Psychological Society (BPS). Only certain accredited psychology degrees will make you eligible for GBR; others may only make you eligible for Graduate Membership of the BPS. Graduate Membership may not make you eligible for a course in forensic psychology and you would need to take a conversion course or a qualifying examination. To find which degree courses are accredited, and for more on conversion courses and qualifying examinations, see Chapter 9 of this book or the careers section of the British Psychological Society website (www.bps.org.uk).

## Work experience

Some form of work in a forensic setting is usually required for those wanting to start a master's course. Note that this experience must be chosen so that it gives you some insight into those who come into contact with the police and court system, and with the range of approaches that are used for punishment and rehabilitation.

You could get suitable experience by working in the prison, probation or social services, perhaps as a psychological assistant or probation service officer. An alternative is to have experience of working in the voluntary sector with offenders or victims, for example with the National Association for the Care and Resettlement of Offenders (NACRO), in bail hostels, refuges, drug and alcohol treatment centres, or with victim support groups. Finally, you could consider working with young people's services (perhaps the regional youth offending service or Connexions) or in health care (for example in a secure hospital or rehabilitation unit).

## Studying psychology at university and school

If you are currently studying at school or college and think you may later wish to become a forensic psychologist, it's worth thinking in advance about how you could most easily progress towards that profession.

Studying psychology at GCSE or A-level will give you a good idea of the basics of the subject. It is also a useful preparation for almost any degree, particularly in subjects such as medicine, the sciences and social sciences. A-level psychology is not a requirement if you want to study the subject at university, though it will be useful. Whatever subjects you choose, however, do remember that you may need to show at least some understanding of the use of scientific methods.

When selecting a psychology course at university, remember that not all of them will give you Graduate Basis for Registration (GBR) of the British Psychological Society (BPS). If you think you may want to work as a forensic psychologist in the future, it is important to apply only for accredited courses.

## Mature students

Since acceptance for training as a forensic psychologist places such an emphasis on practical experience in related fields of work, the training is very suitable for mature students.

If you are thinking of applying as a mature student but are unsure about whether your experience and qualifications are suitable, it will be worthwhile discussing your plans with someone who has experience and knowledge of the British Psychological Society system.

## International applicants

Forensic psychology courses are suitable for people from the UK and other countries that adopt a generally similar approach to the law.

Do remember that preparation for a forensic psychology career involves showing proof of work experience, and that you will need to work in the UK during the two years of the Stage 2 supervised practice. As a result, this is not suitable for people from countries where the legal system is very different from that found in the UK or who require a work permit.

---

### Andrea works as a forensic psychologist in a large prison.

case STUDY

'My interest in working with offenders started rather late. I left school at 16 and went straight into a job in a big retail chain, starting off on the shop floor and then going into junior management. I had to deal with quite a few shoplifters and petty thieves, but thought that was only part of the job.

'I decided that I would need qualifications if I wanted to progress my career. It was a "toss-up" really between a course in management and one in psychology, but in the end psychology seemed more interesting and I thought it might give me more options later.

'My university offered a second-year optional module in criminology and, for some reason, I thought that would be interesting. I think it was that I wanted to see how my psychology degree would relate to practical problems in society. Anyway, it turned out to be fascinating and in the third year I took another optional module on criminology.

'I left university with a 2:1 and a plan to find a career in forensic psychology. My tutor, however, suggested that I should try to get some work experience first, just to check that I really did enjoy the work. Partly with her help I found a six-month placement with NACRO, the organisation that works to rehabilitate offenders. It really made clear to me that offenders need carefully focused help of all sorts of kinds, whether it's practical stuff about finding somewhere to live, working with their drug problem, helping them find work, and so many other things.

'I was tempted to stay with NACRO, but thought it better to get some different experience and so worked for the local Connexions team for the next six months. Both those two types of work experience gave me really useful background before I got a job in a prison as a trainee forensic psychologist and started my master's course.

'My trainee work mainly involved carrying out assessment tests on offenders who may be eligible for early release. It involved giving each individual a series of assessments, analysing the results, and describing and discussing the findings with the rest of the team. Fortunately, I worked closely with the senior forensic psychologist so I got a lot of support.

'The two-year master's course was very good, though combining part-time study with work is hard. I also found the research modules difficult, as much of it was rather new to me. Taking the forensic options in my first degree had meant that I had missed one of the research modules.

'After qualifying in both Part 1 and Part 2 I was awarded the Diploma in Forensic Psychology. That meant that I could progress to more varied work in the prison. I tried to make sure that I got a variety of work, as I think I had always thought of the post as a progression to a more senior position.

'Ten years after my diploma I moved prisons, getting a post as a senior forensic psychologist. I've been there for three years now. It means I supervise both trainee and chartered psychologists and work with senior staff in the prison. I'm also getting involved in plans to change some of our therapeutic approaches, but it needs a lot of research first. I spend quite a lot of time contacting people in other prisons and trying to find out, and analyse, what they do. It would be great if we had limitless funds, but we don't. That makes it all the more important to find out which approaches really work.

'It seems quite a change, from reporting shoplifters to devising plans for offenders. I've enjoyed all the stages of the journey, but I must say that I get the greatest thrill from my current work. It seems to be the way in which I, as just one person, can have the greatest effect.'

## IS THIS THE CAREER FOR ME?

### The practicalities

Work as a forensic psychologist can be stressful since it may involve contact with people who may have committed violent or sexual offences, with distressed victims of crime, or with people having to realise that they will face lengthy periods in prison. There may also be conflicts between the attitudes and practices of, for example, prison staff, social workers and prison visitors. Court work can also be stressful in that lawyers often have the task of trying to question and discredit your professional opinions.

The working hours are mainly nine to five, but some evening and weekend work may be involved. If you become involved with police work, it may be necessary to be available on call in case of emergencies.

Work in large prisons or special hospitals will often be in rural areas, but smaller prisons and other types of forensic work may be based in towns and cities. The psychologist will sometimes have to travel locally to attend meetings or meet colleagues.

Positions with the NHS or the Prison Service may allow some opportunities for other self-employment or freelance work.

## Career prospects

Assistant forensic psychologists typically start at £14,000. While studying for the diploma, trainee forensic psychologists are generally paid in a range from £17,000 to £20,000.

Chartered forensic psychologists generally earn between £26,000 and £38,000, and senior or principal forensic psychologists are generally on scales from £29,000 to £64,000.

At present (2009) the career prospects for forensic psychologists are very good, with a number of vacancies. It's also likely that there will be long-term growth in the provision of psychological and social support for offenders, particularly if this can be shown to reduce the risk of re-offending.

## Self-assessment

In the following sections are brief descriptions of what the job is like in practice, what particular skills and attributes you'll need, and what forensic psychologists find particularly good (and bad) about their work. The comments have deliberately been kept brief so that you can use them as a checklist and assess whether you would suit this career, and whether it would suit you.

## The work in practice

The main tasks for the forensic psychologist are:

- working with a wide range of clients who may have broken the law, who may be violent, may be sex offenders, drug and alcohol users, or may suffer a range of mental health issues

- working as part of a multi-disciplinary team typically including therapists, social workers, prison staff and the police

- using a range of assessment methods to diagnose the problems being experienced by a range of clients

- assessing the risk that an offender may pose if, for example, put on probation or released from prison or a hospital

- advising a range of professionals on specific situations, such as hostage-taking

- selecting and planning a suitable programme of treatment or care for each client, often involving work with other professionals

- carrying out therapeutic work with clients, where there is a match between the client's needs and the forensic psychologist's skills and experience

- carrying out research, generally into the effectiveness of particular therapeutic methods or systems.

## Skills and attributes

The effective forensic psychologist needs particular skills in:

- two-way communication with clients and colleagues

- working both independently and as part of a team

- assessing the risks associated with various offenders

- analysing each client's situation and therapeutic or care needs

- therapeutic skills, and an understanding of when a colleague is better able to offer the skills required

- assessing possible ethical issues, for example relating to confidentiality, equality and diversity

- designing research, carrying it out, analysing the findings and writing a report.

More general attributes include being:

- able to empathise with the client, police, prison officers and other professionals, seeing the situation from their points of view

- knowledgeable about the psychological aspects of the offenders and the law

- emotionally resilient, so that the clients' experiences do not affect your own life

- self-aware, understanding how your own behaviour and attitudes may be affected by your own view of the law and criminals

- an effective team player, able to influence and motivate others

- intellectually rigorous, so that you can investigate and research issues scientifically and produce valid results.

## The highs and lows

Each forensic psychologist will have very different ideas about what aspects of their work they get most from, and which aspects they find most difficult. The following lists show some possible highs and lows.

Highs include:

- seeing an improvement in an offender's attitude and behaviour over an extended period of therapeutic work and rehabilitation

- being accepted by the offender as someone who is prepared to listen and work with them

- working in a team of other professionals

- supervising other professionals and seeing improvement in their practice

- developing training that is then used effectively by fellow professionals

- seeing how the results of your own research can be used to improve the service.

Among the lows are:

- working with abusive, argumentative or resistant offenders

- having to deal with distressing cases

- dealing with the politicking and bureaucracy within the Prison Service

- having a heavy workload, which means that not enough time can be spent on each client

- conflict with fellow professionals (such as prison officers or police officers) who may not have a psychology background and perhaps cannot understand all of the issues

- spending excessive time completing paperwork or recording information on computer systems.

# FINDING OUT MORE

A useful introduction to the subject of forensic psychology can be found in:

- D. Putwain and A. Sammons (2002) *Psychology and Crime.* Routledge.

You can find out more about work as a forensic psychologist on the following websites:

- The British Psychological Society website (www.bps.org.uk), particularly the links to the Division of Forensic Psychology in the Careers and Qualifications section.

- Information on forensic psychology is available at www.all-about -forensic-psychology.com. The website includes a *UK Forensic Psychology Course Directory.*

# Chapter Seven
# OCCUPATIONAL PSYCHOLOGY

Occupational psychologists apply psychological theories and knowledge to the workplace. They typically consider three broad areas of work: how individuals and groups behave in the workplace, what factors affect people's performance and what factors affect the overall performance of the whole organisation.

When working with individuals or groups, the occupational psychologist may focus on how people are affected by their work conditions and the tasks they are required to do. They may also focus on how each person's personality affects their performance and the performance of others in their work group.

Occupational psychologists also work to develop the organisation or to resolve organisational issues. Typical tasks might relate to developing team culture, assessing and developing training programmes, and working to ensure health and safety.

In large organisations, occupational psychologists may be employed to work with management, training officers, trade union representatives, teams and individual staff. Alternatively, occupational psychologists may be employed as consultants, generally focusing on a particular aspect of the organisation.

# WHAT DO OCCUPATIONAL PSYCHOLOGISTS DO?

## Examples from a case load

To get an idea of the work of an occupational psychologist, have a look at some of the brief scenarios below.

- The quality assessors in a large production company are concerned that the quality of work from one team is very poor on Friday afternoons. Most other teams maintain quality quite well. The team's manager contacts the occupational psychologist to ask what he could do about this problem.

- In a company that specialises in finding innovative solutions to IT problems, it's essential that employees can work independently but also work effectively as team members. The occupational psychologist sits on all selection panels to focus specifically on these two requirements and to give her more general assessment of the candidates' suitability.

- The success of a company has meant that all employees have had to do lots of overtime over the past three months. Managers have noticed that there is now an increase in absenteeism and are concerned that it is caused by stress. The occupational psychologist is asked to investigate and, if necessary, suggest solutions.

- During a major economic downturn, staff at a factory have become concerned about the possibility of future redundancies. This is leading to competition between workers and reducing the level of teamwork that senior management have always wanted to encourage. The senior management team and the occupational psychologist discuss their options and agree to hold a series of meetings with workers. The occupational psychologist is asked to draw up a provisional plan for the content of these meetings.

- A major supermarket has always adopted a 'pile 'em high, sell 'em cheap' approach. As a result of its success, there are now many competitors in the market and the company has decided to move its focus onto higher quality and better customer relations. This will need a change in the work culture and a consultant occupational psychologist has been employed to advise on how the organisational culture can most effectively be changed.

As you can see, the work is varied so will need a variety of skills and knowledge. It involves working with managers at all levels, team leaders and supervisors, and all other employees. It requires a wide knowledge of how psychological theory may relate to work. It also requires specific interpersonal skills, skills in assessing and analysing situations and people, and research skills in analysing data and reporting findings.

Finally, it requires self-awareness and an understanding of how you may appear to managers and workers of a wide range of ages, social and educational backgrounds. It may not always be easy to leave a meeting with senior managers and immediately switch to working with a recently appointed school leaver who thinks she is being bullied by her supervisor.

## Eight key knowledge areas

The British Psychological Society has identified eight 'key knowledge areas' relating to occupational psychology. Although not every occupational psychologist will always work in every area, they do give a good idea of the sort of work that you might become involved in.

1  **Human–machine interaction.** How does the operation of a machine affect, for example, the worker's motivation, stress levels or job satisfaction? How can people be selected so that they operate on the particular machines for which they are best suited?

2  **Design of environments and work.** This area relates to two topics. Ergonomics is the study of how efficiently people can use a particular machine or workplace (for example, when using a laptop computer is it better to use a mouse or the touchpad?). Health and safety issues may relate to obviously major issues such as the risk of fire or explosion; but they may also relate to issues like repetitive strain injuries or high levels of stress at work.

**3**  **Personnel selection and assessment.** This includes the design or selection of assessment tests, both for selecting people to work for the organisation and to assess people's skills and knowledge and so help plan their future training and development.

**4**  **Performance appraisal and career development.** Many organisations have a formal system in which managers and individuals appraise the person's past performance, consider future career and work needs, and plan the person's training and development needs for the following year.

**5**  **Personal development and counselling.** As well as working with people's skills and knowledge, occupational psychologists must consider people's personalities and needs. For example, how can people find a suitable balance between their work and other needs, and so create a suitable work–life balance? What help can the organisation provide to those who are experiencing personal difficulties?

**6**  **Training.** This area of work relates to three main tasks. The first is to identify the specific training needs of teams and individuals. The second then involves either selecting a suitable training course, or designing one to fit the specific need. The third involves evaluating the course itself and the effects it has had on performance, so that further training can be planned where necessary.

**7**  **Employee relations and motivation.** This area of knowledge relates to virtually all of the preceding areas, and is perhaps the key aspect that underlies all occupational psychology work.

**8**  **Organisational development and change.** This area also relates to many of the other areas. Organisational development work involves considering the organisation, its teams and individuals from many perspectives, and planning and implementing change at many levels. This aspect of occupational psychology is perhaps the most challenging, involving both wide-ranging changes and specific change programmes relating perhaps to one or two employees.

## Unemployment

A further area of occupational psychology relates to unemployment, looking at how people may cope with unemployment, redundancy, retirement or job-seeking. The psychologist working in an organisation, or as a consultant, where there is a threat of redundancies may need to investigate how workers may identify alternatives to unemployment, or cope with redeployment, changing jobs or changing work locations. If people are to be made redundant, they may need advice on how to use their future leisure time, and may need counselling on practical or emotional issues.

## Management–worker relations

Occupational psychologists also become involved in wider issues of industrial relations. They may be asked to advise on negotiations with trade unions, and on pay and incentive schemes. As with many aspects of human resources work, the emphasis is on creating effective relationships between management and employees.

## Work settings

Many occupational psychologists work in human resources departments. They may have the job title occupational psychologist, or may work on specific aspects of the work, for example working in training and development, ergonomics, or health and safety.

Consultant occupational psychologists may offer a similar range of services, or may offer specific skills, for example relating to encouraging emotional intelligence, psychometric testing, psychological profiling, conflict resolution, or executive coaching.

The work is generally from nine to five, though consultants may need to work at weekends or evenings when marketing services or delivering training. Occupational psychologists working in organisations that operate from more than one site may need to travel between sites.

# ENTRY REQUIREMENTS

Provided you have a suitable degree in psychology, there are two stages to becoming a chartered occupational psychologist.

The first stage is to take an accredited master's course in occupational psychology. You can find suitable courses on the BPS website (www. bps.org.uk). This will generally be a one-year full-time course or a two-year part-time course.

The second stage involves two years of supervised work experience in the workplace. Completing the two stages successfully will qualify you for a Qualification in Occupational Psychology (QOccPsych). You can then register as a chartered occupational psychologist and gain full membership of the British Psychological Society Division of Occupational Psychology.

You need to check that your first degree gives you Graduate Basis for Registration (GBR) of the British Psychological Society (BPS). Only certain accredited psychology degrees will make you eligible for GBR; others may only make you eligible for Graduate Membership of the BPS. Graduate Membership may not make you eligible for a course in occupational psychology and you would need to take a conversion course or a qualifying examination. To find out which degree courses are accredited, and for more on conversion courses and qualifying examinations, see Chapter 9 of this book or the careers section of the British Psychological Society website (www.bps.org.uk).

## Studying psychology at university and school

If you are currently studying at school or college and think you may later wish to become an occupational psychologist, it's worth thinking in advance how you could most easily progress towards that profession.

Studying psychology at GCSE or A-level will give you a good idea of the basics of the subject. It is also a useful preparation for almost any degree, particularly in subjects such as medicine, the sciences and social sciences. A-level psychology is not a requirement if you want to study the subject at university, though it will be useful. Whatever subjects you choose, however, do remember that you may need to show at least some understanding of the use of scientific methods.

When selecting a psychology course at university, it may be useful to take a joint-honours course that combines psychology with business studies, or focuses on applied psychology. However, remember that not all courses will give you Graduate Basis for Registration (GBR) of the British Psychological Society (BPS). If you think you may want to work as an occupational psychologist in the future, it is important to apply only for accredited courses.

## Mature students

Acceptance for training as an occupational psychologist is easier if you have some relevant previous experience, perhaps of work in a human resources or training department. It is common for mature adults to study on occupational psychologist courses. Thinking of what occupational psychology involves, you will also realise that some degree of maturity and self-knowledge is needed if you are to work with the wide range of people that you will meet in the workplace, and if you are to work effectively to influence other professionals.

If you are thinking of applying as a mature student but are unsure about whether your experience and qualifications are suitable, it will be worthwhile contacting the relevant university to find out whether or not your particular experience is relevant.

## What non-academic skills do I need?

Apart from academic qualifications, as an occupational psychologist you will need to be an excellent communicator with sensitivity, tact and diplomacy, coupled with the ability to be assertive, persuasive and an effective facilitator. You must also possess strong negotiating, administration and time management skills. You'll also need effective research skills if you are to collect data on organisational issues, analyse the data, form conclusions and plan future actions.

## Work experience

Occupational psychology relates to a very wide range of skills and knowledge. You could have relevant experience from working in fields relating, for example, to human resource management, careers guidance, counselling or care, disability or equality issues, or running your own business.

Mature graduates may also find that they have relevant experience linked to roles in management or from work in any organisation that involves interaction with managers and employees.

It may be possible to find work as an assistant occupational psychologist, and to build on that experience through further study for a part-time master's course.

## International applicants

Potential students from outside the UK will need to contact the British Psychological Society to gain confirmation that their first degree is recognised.

If you come from a non-EU country you will also need to consider how you can complete the work experience element of qualifying for the chartered status.

**Mark works for a large multi-national company which has its headquarters in the south of England, with other offices throughout Europe and some production departments in south-east Asia.**

'I knew from an early age that I wanted to work with people, and by my mid-teens had decided that I wanted to become a psychologist. I took GCSE and A-level psychology and found that the ideas seemed to be really useful when I worked in the local supermarket at holidays and weekends. You could see how a lot of the people found the work really boring and so they couldn't be bothered to do it well. Then we got a new manager and she somehow managed to motivate people. It wasn't anything specific; she just seemed to change the mood in the place.

'I did a joint honours course that combined psychology and business studies. The lecturers also gave every student help in getting work experience in the long vacations, and I got placements in three very varied companies. I also tried to get some experience working on the shop floor as well as in human relations departments.

'After my degree I was unsure exactly what area of work I wanted to go into, so I got a job working for a publisher that develops assessment tests. It gave me really useful background into how the tests are developed, the situations in which they can be valid, and the limits on their validity. I also visited lots of companies and met lots of consultants during the research stages and as part of our marketing process. I worked for the publishers for three years before I decided that I was ready to take the occupational psychology course.

'I took the master's course as a part-time student, combining it with my publishing work. That got me my Stage 1 and helped me to get my next job, in the human relations department in my present company. They already had a chartered occupational psychologist and he supervised my work experience for the next two years so that I qualified for Stage 2 and qualified for chartered status myself.

'Quite a lot of people move soon after qualifying, but I decided to stay where I was and benefit more from my supervisor's experience. In the end I stayed for five years, working in pretty well all the eight areas that the BPS lists, and also developing new policies to do with equality and diversity. My boss retired and I took over his role as senior occupational psychologist; I'm currently supervising my replacement while she works towards chartered status.

'What are the best bits of the job? I suppose it's trying to be like that old supermarket manager and seeing how creating a happy workforce is good for people and for the business.'

# IS THIS THE CAREER FOR ME?

## The practicalities

The working hours are mainly nine to five, but some evening and weekend work may be involved, for example if some employees work shifts. If you work for a multi-location organisation you will have some travelling between sites. Consultant occupational psychologists may spend considerable time travelling to their client companies.

Most positions exist in large towns and cities and you may have to work on a large industrial site. Most consultancies are based in the south-east of England.

The work can be stressful since it often involves conflict, for example between groups of workers, or between management and workers. Occupational psychologists also come up against the practical situations in which there are entrenched positions, typically based on events in the organisation's history.

Part-time working is possible and may allow other self-employment or freelance work. For example, an occupational psychologist working part-time for an organisation may also set up a consultancy. This has benefits for the individual, but the wider experience may also create benefits for the employing organisation.

## Career prospects

Typical salary ranges are currently (2009):

- trainee occupational psychologist: £15,000 to £20,000
- chartered occupational psychologist: £20,000 to £30,000
- senior occupational psychologist: £30,000 to £70,000.

At present the career prospects for occupational psychologists are good. However, the current downturn in the economy may make employment prospects in the short term more difficult.

## Career progression

The skills and knowledge gained in training as an occupational psychologist can be used in many other roles in organisations, from relatively low-level posts up the senior management.

Occupational psychologists also have the option of moving into specialist areas, such as ergonomics, training or conflict prevention. The scope for consultancy work is wide, with many organisations using consultants to supply expertise in rapidly developing or specialist aspects of human resource work.

## Self-assessment

In the following sections are brief descriptions of what the job is like in practice, what particular skills and attributes you'll need, and what occupational psychologists find particularly good (and bad) about their work. The comments have deliberately been kept brief so that you can use them as a checklist and assess whether you would suit this career, and whether it would suit you.

## The work in practice

The main tasks are:

- working with a wide range of employees, supervisors and managers at all levels

- researching specific work situations, forming conclusions, making recommendations and planning interventions

- working as part of a multi-disciplinary human resources team to plan, for example, organisational change, and training and development

- developing and reviewing policies as they relate to the personal experiences of people at work

- studying the human–machine interactions in the workplace and planning ways of maximising efficiency and effectiveness, while also ensuring the health and safety of all people in the workplace

- working to ensure the effective recruitment, selection and development of the workforce

- helping individuals through personal development programmes and work-based counselling

- writing reports to make formal recommendations on action to be taken.

## Skills and attributes

The effective occupational psychologist needs particular skills in:

- two-way communication with employees, supervisors and management at all levels

- analysing work situations and planning effective interventions

- working both independently and as part of a team

- advising, negotiating, persuading and supporting employees, managers and other human resource professionals

- planning, implementing and assessing training and change programmes

- assessing possible ethical issues, for example relating to confidentiality, equality and diversity.

More general attributes include being:

- experienced in a wide range of work situations

- able to empathise with the employees and management, seeing the situation from their various points of view

- effective in meetings and discussions with all employees, managers and other human resource professionals

- able to stand back from an emotional response to a work situation and rigorously evaluate the possible courses of future action

- self-aware, understanding how your own behaviour and attitudes may affect other people in the workplace

- patient; many work situations are a result of historical factors which may take some time to overcome

- an effective team player, able to influence and motivate others

- self-motivating, able to work independently, sometimes in difficult and challenging situations

■ intellectually rigorous, so that you can investigate and research issues scientifically and produce valid results.

## The highs and lows

Each occupational psychologist will have very different ideas about what aspects of their work they get most from, and which aspects they find most difficult. The following lists show some possible highs and lows.

Highs include:

■ seeing an improvement in a workplace or in the behaviour or attitudes of individual workers or groups

■ being accepted by both sides in a conflict situation as someone who is prepared to listen and work with them

■ working with a varied range of people at all levels of the organisation

■ having varied work so that no two days are ever the same

■ having the freedom to work independently

■ seeing the benefits of training or organisational change that you have developed

■ seeing how the results of your own research can be used to improve people's experience or output at work.

Among the lows are:

■ working with people, whether employees or managers, who refuse to change their views or compromise

■ working with people who are being made redundant

■ having a case load that is overloaded with assessments, giving little time to plan interventions and programmes

■ having to 'sell' the benefits of human resource or occupational psychology skills to managers

■ spending excessive time on bureaucratic processes, completing paperwork or recording information on computer systems.

# FINDING OUT MORE

There are a number of textbooks that introduce occupational psychology. Skim-reading one of the following texts will give you a feel for the subject:

- Millward, L.J. (2005) *Understanding Occupational & Organizational Psychology.* Sage.

- Rothmann, I. and Cooper, C. (2008) *Organizational and Work Psychology: Topics in Applied Psychology.* Hodder Arnold.

You can find out more about work as an occupational psychologist on the following websites:

- the British Psychological Society website www.bps.org.uk particularly the Careers and Qualifications section

- the People and Organisations at Work website of the British Psychological Society (www.pow-bps.com)

- the Chartered Institute of Personnel and Development (www.cipd. co.uk).

You can also inspect a free copy of the *Journal of Occupational and Organisational Psychology* by searching for that title on the British Psychological Society website www.bps.org.uk

# Chapter Eight
# HEALTH, SPORT AND EXERCISE PSYCHOLOGY

This chapter describes two psychologist roles, both of which relate physical health and psychology.

Health psychologists work to prevent mental and physical illness by encouraging people to follow healthy lifestyles. Typical areas of work include explaining the risks of smoking, encouraging safe-sex methods, or explaining the importance of skincare in the sun. They also work with people who have had major accidents or have been diagnosed with serious illness, such as cancer or AIDS. Their work will typically also involve research into the effectiveness of healthy-living programmes or into the various coping strategies that clients may use.

Sport and exercise psychologists use psychological theory to maximise the performance of sportspeople and to encourage the wider population to exercise effectively. A key element of this role is to work with individuals, planning their goals and the process by which they hope to achieve them. It also involves working with people as they experience the inevitable problems and difficulties, and helping to overcome them. Sport and exercise psychologists may also become involved in education (in sports centres or in the wider community) and in research, for example to assess the effectiveness of exercise or education programmes.

In the following pages you will find descriptions of the two roles.

# WHAT DO HEALTH PSYCHOLOGISTS DO?

## Examples from a case load

To get an idea of the work of a health psychologist, have a look at some of the brief scenarios below.

- The health psychologist worked at a local secondary school during their 'Anti-Smoking Day'. The day included a short film on the dangers of smoking, followed by a question and answer session in which the health psychologist was able to give more detailed information on the risks.

- Dave is a cancer patient who has recently had to stop work because of his illness. After a meeting with Dave, the health psychologist arranged for him to meet a counsellor (to help him deal with the emotional effects of his illness) and a social worker, who would help with the practical issues raised by his disability.

- A local mental health centre had become concerned about stress levels experienced by some of its staff, many of whom worked with particularly difficult clients. The health psychologist was asked to investigate the problem. She recommended that she should offer short-term programmes in stress management for individual workers. She also recommended that longer-term therapeutic counselling and support should be available to those who requested it, and was involved in the selection of a suitable therapist.

- The health psychologist also kept records of all interviews and interventions at the mental health centre. After the programme had been running for two years, she carried out further study to investigate its success. She wrote up her findings and published a summary that could be helpful to others working in the field.

As you can see, the work is varied so will require a variety of skills and knowledge. It involves working with a range of other professionals, mainly in the areas of health, social care and education. It also involves working with clients who may be experiencing emotional trauma, for example after a major accident or a diagnosis of serious illness or disability.

It requires a wide knowledge of how psychological theory may relate to people's reactions to illness. It also requires specific interpersonal skills, skills in assessing and analysing situations and people, and research skills in analysing data and reporting findings.

## Work settings

Health psychologists may work in a range of medical settings, such as hospitals, rehabilitation centres or large GP practices. Those who focus on research will typically be employed in government health research units, health authorities or universities.

The work is generally from nine to five, though health promotion activities may involve evening or weekend work. Health psychologists working in organisations that operate from more than one site may need to travel between sites.

# WHAT DO SPORT AND EXERCISE PSYCHOLOGISTS DO?

## Examples from a case load

To get an idea of the work of sport and exercise psychologists, have a look at some of the brief scenarios below. Do note that people tend to specialise in one or other of the two areas.

### Sport psychologist

- The manager of a professional football team was concerned that the team was underperforming, but was unsure about the causes. The sport psychologist was employed as a consultant to investigate the situation. After identifying one major issue as the difficulties of communicating in a team drawn from many nationalities, he was employed to work on communication skills and to build team cohesion.

- Jane Spencer had won the Junior World Championship in squash but was concerned that she would not have the self-confidence to succeed as a senior. The sports psychologist employed by the

National Squash Association was asked to work with her on this issue as she progressed to the senior level.

■ An enthusiastic amateur skier, John Powell is concerned that a recent accident has damaged his confidence. 'I'm still OK technically, but I don't seem to be able to "go for it" as I used to do.' He visits a sports psychologist to discuss how he can overcome his fear of having another accident.

## Exercise psychologist

■ The manager of a local sports centre is concerned that, although large numbers of people sign up for exercise classes, there is a very high drop-out rate. He asks the exercise psychologist employed by the chain of sports centres to study the problem. The psychologist suggests that each person signing up for a course should initially meet a centre coach, discuss their programme, and assess progress at a series of regular meetings.

■ Some of the fitness instructors at the same centre talk about how difficult it is to maintain their enthusiasm with certain groups. In a meeting with the exercise psychologist they discuss the problem and he suggests some techniques which they can use to maintain their own levels of enthusiasm. They agree to meet again in a month's time to assess whether the techniques have been helpful and to plan how they can further improve.

■ The exercise psychologist is asked to take part in a 'Healthy Living Day' at a local college. She notes that a number of students are very active sportspeople, but that the majority do very little exercise. During her work with the young people she is careful to emphasise both the physical and the psychological benefits of exercise. She also emphasises that exercise need not involve competitive sports.

As you can see, the work is varied so will need a variety of skills and knowledge. It involves working with a range of other professionals, typically including team managers, exercise instructors and physiotherapists.

Sports psychologists will often work with clients who have strong personalities. Professional sportspeople may earn considerably more than the psychologist, and may have succeeded in part because they have a strong self-image. There may also be the additional challenge of working with these strong personalities in relation to teamwork.

Exercise psychology may involve working with clients who enjoy their exercise and simply need a little more motivation. On the other hand, it may involve work with those who have done little exercise for years and who are reluctantly starting exercise, for example after being told they have heart disease or a similar health problem.

Both sport and exercise psychology require a wide knowledge of how psychological theory may relate to people's motivation, their reactions to success or the lack of it, reactions to physical problems, and so on. It also requires strong interpersonal skills, skills in assessing and analysing situations and people.

## Work settings

Sport and exercise psychologists may work in a range of sport and fitness settings, such as sports centres and universities, or for professional sports teams and sports associations. It is quite likely that sport psychologists will work on a part-time or consultancy basis; exercise psychologists are more likely to work on a full-time basis for a specific organisation.

The role often involves evening and weekend work.

# ENTRY REQUIREMENTS

Provided you have a suitable degree in psychology, there are two stages to becoming a chartered health psychologist or chartered sport and exercise psychologist.

The first stage is to take an accredited master's course in either health psychology or sport and exercise psychology. You can find suitable courses on the BPS website (www.bps.org.uk). This will generally be a one-year full-time course or a two-year part-time course.

The second stage involves two years of supervised work experience in the workplace. Completing the two stages successfully will qualify you for a Qualification in Health Psychology (QHP) or a Qualification in Sport and Exercise Psychology (QSEP). You can then register as a Chartered Health Psychologist or a Chartered Sport and Exercise Psychologist and gain full membership of the Health Psychology Division or Sport and Exercise Division of the British Psychological Society.

You need to check that your first degree gives you Graduate Basis for Registration (GBR) of the British Psychological Society (BPS). Only certain accredited psychology degrees will make you eligible for GBR; others may only make you eligible for Graduate Membership of the BPS. Graduate Membership may not make you eligible for a further course in health or sports and exercise psychology and you would need to take a conversion course or a qualifying examination. To find out which degree courses are accredited, and for more on conversion courses and qualifying examinations, see Chapter 9 of this book or the careers section of the British Psychological Society website (www. bps.org.uk).

## Studying psychology at university and school

If you are currently studying at school or college and think you may later wish to become a health psychologist or a sport or exercise psychologist, it's worth thinking in advance how you could most easily progress towards that profession.

Studying psychology at GCSE or A-level will give you a good idea of the basics of the subject. It is also a useful preparation for almost any degree, particularly in subjects such as medicine, the sciences and social sciences. A-level psychology is not a requirement if you want to study the subject at university, though it will be useful. Whatever subjects you choose, however, do remember that you may need to show at least some understanding of the use of scientific methods.

When selecting an undergraduate psychology course at university, you could follow a general psychology course or follow a course specifically in health psychology or in sport and exercise psychology. However, remember that not all courses will give you Graduate Basis for Registration (GBR) of the British Psychological Society (BPS). If you think you may want to work as a chartered psychologist in the future, it is important to apply only for accredited courses.

## Mature students

As a health psychologist, you will need good interpersonal skills if you are to effectively work to persuade people to adopt a more healthy lifestyle. You will also need some of the skills of a counsellor if you are going to help people to come to terms with the effects of a major accident, illness or disability. For both of these reasons, mature students are welcomed onto health psychology courses.

Acceptance for training as a sports or exercise psychologist requires enthusiasm for sport and exercise. It is thus suitable for those who want to change from a career in sport. Do note that the work will involve using significant interpersonal skills when working to motivate people or to help them to overcome injury of lack of self-confidence.

If you are thinking of applying as a mature student but are unsure about whether your experience and qualifications are suitable, it will be worthwhile contacting the relevant university to find out whether or not your particular experience is relevant.

## What non-academic skills do I need?

Apart from academic qualifications, health, sport and exercise psychologists need to be excellent communicators, often need to be assertive and persuasive, and need to show sensitivity, tact and diplomacy. You will also need to possess strong administration and time management skills, particularly if you work as a consultant or in a number of part-time roles.

If you choose to work as a health psychologist you'll need effective research skills if you are to collect data, analyse the data, form conclusions and plan future actions.

## Work experience

Students wanting to follow sport and exercise courses will need to show considerable experience and interest, often in a range of sports (for example, involving both individual and team sports). Playing a particular sport, having training qualifications or working in a sports centre may give useful experience.

Those wanting to study health psychology may need to show experience in working in a related aspect of health care, for example working in a rehabilitation centre, with disabled people, or in a sports centre. Experience in nursing or social care may be relevant.

## International applicants

Potential students from outside the UK will need to contact the British Psychological Society to gain confirmation that their first degree is recognised.

If you come from a non-EU country you will also need to consider how you can complete the work experience element of qualifying for the Chartered status.

### Sheila says that she has always been fascinated by sport and sportspeople.

She played a lot of different sports from an early age, but by the time she was 12 she had settled on tennis and hockey as her main interests. She played both sports for her county junior squads. 'I was probably better at hockey really, but thought that tennis was the only way I was going to manage to play sport professionally.'

At the age of 16, Sheila, her tennis coach and her parents sat down and discussed possible careers. The coach was quite realistic and said that she just possibly might reach the top level, but that it was only a slim chance.

Sheila decided to work to get into university, while still playing both sports for local clubs. To keep contact with her tennis coach she went to a local university and played both tennis and hockey for university teams, and the local clubs when she could. The university offered a course in psychology, with options that allowed Sheila to focus on sport and exercise psychology in years 2 and 3.

By the time Sheila reached the second year, she realised that a career as a tennis player was not going to be possible. She took coaching courses in tennis and hockey and got some practice coaching local children and adults. 'Rather to my surprise, I found that coaching was not really what I wanted to do. I found the repetition of teaching specific skills to young players could become tedious. It was much more interesting to work with adults on the mental side of their game.'

After completing her psychology degree, Sheila moved to a larger university to take a two-year part-time master's course in sport and exercise psychology. She combined her study with work as a coach in a sports centre. After completing the course, she was accepted as a research assistant in the university and is currently working towards a doctorate in psychology, focusing on the problems that can face sportspeople recovering from injury. She combines her study and university work with consultancy work at the same sports centre.

'I'm really glad that I moved from coaching to sport psychology. My work is very varied. My research work is based on a highly specialised area of sports psychology, but I also get a chance to work with a number of people, from the adult returning to sport in midlife to athletes working at quite high levels in their sport. I'm also hoping that I will soon get to work with students studying sport and exercise psychology.'

# IS THIS THE CAREER FOR ME?

## The practicalities

The working hours of health psychologists are mainly nine to five, though there may be some health promotion work in the evenings and weekends. Most positions exist in large towns and cities.

Part-time working is possible and may allow other self-employment or freelance work. For example, a health psychologist working part-time for a local health care trust organisation may also set up a consultancy. This has benefits for the individual, but the wider experience may also create benefits for the employing organisation.

Sport and exercise psychologists, in contrast, may need to work extensively at weekends or evenings. Most positions exist in large towns and cities.

Many sport and exercise psychologists combine work at a university, health or sports centre with self-employment or freelance work. For example, an exercise psychologist working part-time for a local fitness centre may also set up a consultancy working with individuals who want to follow an exercise programme.

## Career prospects

Typical salary ranges for health psychologists are currently (2009) in the range £20,000 to £30,000, with those in senior posts earning up to £40,000.

The career prospects for health psychologists are good, with an increasing government focus on the benefits of healthy lifestyles and exercise. There is also an increased realisation of the importance of developing coping strategies following accidents or the development of long-term illness. Finally, there is an increasing focus on research into how to encourage people to exercise, and into how people best cope with illness or injury.

Typical salary ranges for sport and exercise psychologists are more difficult to assess, since they may work in a wide range of settings. Lecturers working in FE colleges can expect to earn in the range £17,000 to £25,500, with increases to £37,000 for senior posts. Lecturers in universities can expect to earn roughly 25% above those figures. Levels of pay for sport psychologists working full-time or as consultants in various sports will vary widely, largely depending on the particular sport.

The career prospects for sport and exercise psychologists are good, with an increasing public awareness of healthy lifestyles and exercise.

There is also an increasing awareness of the benefits of exercise throughout life, rather than it being restricted to the young. There is also an increasing focus on research into assessing the effectiveness of different approaches to exercise and its promotion.

## Career progression

The skills and knowledge gained in training as a health psychologist, or a sport and exercise psychologist, can be used in certain other roles in related organisations, from relatively low-level posts up to senior management. There is also the possibility of moving from one sector to another, for example moving from a role as a health psychologist in the NHS to a role in a large commercial organisation.

The scope for consultancy work is wide, with many organisations using consultants to supply expertise in promoting healthy lifestyles, encouraging individuals to exercise, or to motivate sportspeople at all levels.

## Self-assessment: health psychologist

In the following section are brief descriptions of what the role of the health psychologist is like in practice, what particular skills and attributes you'll need, and what health psychologists find particularly good (and bad) about their work. The comments have deliberately been kept brief so that you can use them as a checklist and assess whether you would suit this career, and whether it would suit you.

This self-assessment is followed by a similar self-assessment for the role of sport and exercise psychologist.

## The work of the health psychologist in practice

The main tasks are:

- providing psychological and practical help to individuals who have experienced major accidents, are recovering from major surgery or have been diagnosed as having major illness

- working with a wide range of professionals from the field of health and social care, including surgeons, GPs, physiotherapists, care workers and others

- working with those involved in health promotion, including researchers, publicity and media officers, and fitness and exercise providers

- working as part of a multi-disciplinary team to plan, for example, the care of a post-operative patient or a person with a disability or major illness

- researching specific health promotion approaches, forming conclusions and making recommendations

- writing reports to make formal recommendations on action to be taken.

## Skills and attributes

The effective health psychologist needs particular skills in:

- two-way communication with clients, professionals and management at all levels

- analysing distressing health situations and planning effective interventions

- working both independently and as part of a team

- planning, implementing and assessing psychological and practical assistance

- assessing possible ethical issues, for example relating to confidentiality, equality and diversity.

More general attributes include being:

- patient and caring

- able to appear optimistic and positive

- able to empathise with the seriously injured and the long-term or terminally ill, seeing the situation from their various points of view

- able to stand back from an emotional response to a work situation and rigorously evaluate the possible courses of future action

- self-aware, understanding how your own behaviour and attitudes may affect the various patients

- intellectually rigorous, so that you can investigate and research issues scientifically and produce valid results.

## The highs and lows

Each health psychologist will have very different ideas about what aspects of their work they get most from, and which aspects they find most difficult. The following lists show some possible highs and lows.

Highs include:

- seeing an improvement in an individual's reactions to illness or injury

- seeing the benefits to a patient of a particular health programme

- seeing the positive effect of a health promotion

- working with a varied range of people at all levels of the organisation

- having varied work so that no two days are ever the same

- having the freedom to work independently

- seeing how the results of your own research can be used to improve people's health.

Among the lows are:

- seeing the steady decline in health of individual patients

- working with people who are very ill or disabled

- having an overloaded case load

- spending excessive time on bureaucratic processes, completing paperwork or recording information on computer systems.

## Self-assessment: sport and exercise psychologist

In the following section are brief descriptions of what the role of the sport and exercise psychologist is like in practice, what particular skills and attributes you'll need, and what sport and exercise psychologists find particularly good (and bad) about their work. The comments have deliberately been kept brief so that you can use them as a checklist and assess whether you would suit this career, and whether it would suit you.

## The work of the sport and exercise psychologist in practice

The main tasks are:

- working with a wide range of clients, each with specific aims and needs

- motivating individuals and groups to become involved in exercise

- working with a range of other sport and exercise professionals, such as coaches, nutritionists, physical education teachers and trainers

- teaching specific skills such as relaxation, visualisation and positive self-belief

- developing and reviewing organisational policies as they relate to health and exercise

- researching specific aspects of sport or exercise, such as the effectiveness of particular techniques or approaches to promotion

- writing reports to make formal recommendations on action to be taken.

## Skills and attributes

The effective sport and exercise psychologist needs particular skills in:

- motivating individuals to adopt particular approaches or attitudes

- two-way communication with clients and management at all levels

- analysing sport or exercise situations and planning effective interventions

- working both independently and as part of a team

- advising, negotiating, persuading and supporting those who work on or provide exercise programmes

- planning, implementing and assessing programmes to assess sport or exercise interventions

- assessing possible ethical issues, for example relating to confidentiality, equality and diversity.

More general attributes include being:

- experienced in a wide range of sport and exercise

- able to inspire clients though your own personality and specific motivational techniques

- able to empathise with clients, seeing the situation from their various points of view

- effective in meetings and discussions with those who provide sport and exercise facilities

- self-aware, understanding how your own behaviour and attitudes may affect your clients

- patient; many sport and exercise situations involve deep-seated attitudes which may take some time to overcome

- an effective team player, able to influence and motivate others

- self-motivating, able to work independently, sometimes with sceptical individuals or their coaches.

## The highs and lows

Each sport and exercise psychologist will have very different ideas about what aspects of their work they get most from, and which aspects they find most difficult. The following lists show some possible highs and lows.

Highs include:

- seeing an improvement in a sportsperson's performance, or the attitude of a person to exercise

- working with highly motivated people

- using, and sharing the benefits of, your own experiences in sport

- working with a varied range of people at all levels of the organisation

- working with a varied group of clients

- having the freedom to work independently

- seeing the benefits of a training programme that you have developed

- seeing how the results of your own research can be used to improve people's experience of exercise or training.

Among the lows are:

- working with people, whether clients or coaches, who refuse to change their views or compromise

- working with people who do not reach the standard they hope to achieve

- working with managers, coaches or individuals who have unrealistic ideas of what sport or exercise psychology can achieve

- having to 'sell' the benefits of exercise to clients, or of sport psychology to coaches and sportspeople.

## FINDING OUT MORE

There are a number of textbooks that introduce health psychology. Skim-reading one of the following texts, or similar texts that you can find in your library, will give you a feel for each subject area:

- Ogden, J. (2007) *Health Psychology.* Oxford University Press.

- Moran, A.P. (2003) *Sport and Exercise Psychology Textbook: A Critical Introduction.* Routledge.

You can find out more about work as a health psychologist or a sport and exercise psychologist on the following websites:

■　the British Psychological Society website, www.bps.org.uk, accessing particularly the *Careers and Qualifications* section, the Division of Health Psychology, and the Division of Sport and Exercise Psychology

■　the British Association for Sport and Exercise Sciences (www.bases.org.uk).

# Chapter Nine
# **TRAINING, SKILLS AND QUALIFICATIONS**

This chapter looks at the skills, knowledge and qualifications that you can gain from a study of psychology at different levels, from GCSE and A-level, from a psychology degree, from postgraduate study, and from supervised work experience leading to accreditation as a chartered psychologist.

As you can see, the process follows a series of steps, each leading to progressively narrower career choices. In practice, fewer than 20% of psychology graduates complete all the steps and go on to chartered status. This chapter will also describe the various options that are available at each of the steps we describe. For example:

■ what other degree courses will accept you if you have A-level psychology

■ what careers in public or commercial organisations are available if you have a degree in psychology

■ what value does qualification in other subjects have – for example, would you be accepted for a master's in psychology if you had originally taken a degree in nursing or education?

# PSYCHOLOGY AT SCHOOL AND COLLEGE

Psychology can be taken at GCSE and A-level. You can also use the S/NVQ approach to study, measure and demonstrate your understanding of psychology.

While these courses are not essential if you want to study for a degree in psychology, they will give you a useful picture of what psychology involves, and may help you to make a decision about your future study or career.

## What skills will I gain by studying psychology?

Studying psychology gives you a very wide range of skills.

- As a science it develops skills in numeracy and the analysis of mathematical data, the ability to analyse information, and requires you to develop skills of forming conclusions, stating recommendations and reporting on your findings.

- Rather like a student in the humanities, a psychology student also develops skills such as critical thinking and essay writing.

- Working with individuals you develop two-way communication skills, learning how to listen and observe, and how to explain and persuade.

- Working in teams you learn more interpersonal skills, observe the ways in which people interact and practise interacting with others.

- The studying process itself teaches you a number of skills linked to information technology – for example, how to use a spreadsheet or word processing package, search for and access information on the web, and use display tools to present your thoughts and findings to others.

## What are my choices after school or college?

After studying at school or college, you have three broad options if you think you want to continue your study of psychology.

First, a degree in psychology will further increase the skills and knowledge that you gained from your study at school or college. After three or four years' study you will be qualified to enter a wide range of careers. A number of the ones that will most directly use your skills in psychology are described in Chapter 2, under the headings 'Health and social care', 'Community work', 'Education' and 'Organisational roles'.

Second, if you have a clear idea of which field of psychology you find most interesting, you could apply for a degree in that field. There are, for example, a number of degrees with titles such as forensic psychology, sport and exercise psychology, or occupational psychology.

Finally, many psychology degrees, and all further qualifications leading to chartered status, require experience in a variety of work situations. On a more practical note, you are much more likely to understand some of the theory you meet at university if you have practical experience of some of the psychological issues. You may find it really useful to take a year out after school or college so that you can work in, say, a voluntary organisation, a local health centre, a prison or young person's institution, a rehabilitation centre, or the human resources department of a large organisation.

## What if I'm returning to study after some years at work?

Many mature students study psychology at university after a period in the workplace. The range of qualifications and experiences that mature students bring is very wide, so it is difficult to generalise about what they need to do to continue their studies.

However, if you have school or college qualifications and work experience you will find that many universities will give weight to your experience and maturity, even if you do not have all of the normally required paper qualifications. If you have not studied for some time, the university may require you to follow an introductory programme in study skills.

# UNIVERSITY COURSES IN PSYCHOLOGY

## How do I get accepted for a psychology degree course?

The minimum requirements for a degree course are normally two A-levels and five GCSEs at grade C or better, or equivalent qualifications such as NVQs or SVQs. There is not generally a formal requirement to have studied psychology, though many universities will expect you to be able to show that you have some experience of working with scientific concepts and have writing skills.

The actual requirements for a particular degree vary widely, depending on the particular course and the university. There is often strong competition for psychology degrees at the major universities. Most university websites give information on the typical grades that they will accept. Note, also, that universities may be more likely to accept candidates with additional work or study experience.

## Mature students

Increasingly, universities are accepting evidence of previous study or work experience as qualifications for entry onto a degree course. If you are a mature student with relevant experience, you should refer to the university department website to find out more about its selection policies.

It is possible to begin training as a psychologist at any age, but note that the process of becoming a chartered psychologist will typically involve three years for a first degree, a further one to three years for a master's or doctorate qualification, and perhaps three years' work experience.

## What topics will I study?

The content of psychology degree courses varies depending on the course title and the university. However, all courses accredited by the British Psychological Society must include modules on the following topics.

- **Biological** psychology, studying how the brain works, the effects of hormones and drugs, and the treatment of biologically based mental disorders.

- **Cognitive** psychology, looking at how we remember, learn, think, reason, perceive, speak and understand.

- **Developmental** psychology, studying the ways in which humans develop physically, mentally and socially.

- **Social** psychology, investigating how behaviour and attitudes may be affected by families, peers and the wider society.

- **Personality**, looking at why people have different personalities and aptitudes.

- **The development of psychological concepts**, considering the ways in which the study of psychology has developed over time.

- **Research methods**, covering the design of experiments, collection of data, analysis, and the formation of conclusions.

All courses will also include optional elements that you can study to find out about particular aspects of psychology, for example in the application of psychology in the workplace, the psychology of education, sport psychology and so on.

## What careers are available if I have a degree?

As you saw in Chapter 2, many careers are available to graduates with psychology degrees. The figure on the next page shows some examples under the four headings: 'Health and social care', 'Community work', 'Education' and 'Organisational roles'.

Most of these examples do not involve further academic study, but some will involve knowledge and experience in specific topics. For example, working in outdoor education typically needs qualifications in areas such as canoeing or rock-climbing.

Note that the skills acquired during a psychology degree will also qualify you for a very wide range of other careers. For example, research skills may be relevant to research work in a very wide range of organisations and industries, and skills in mathematics and analysis will be relevant to further training in accountancy or market research.

# POSTGRADUATE STUDY IN PSYCHOLOGY

## Routes to becoming a psychologist

University degree courses vary in the depth to which you can study a particular aspect of psychology. For example, you could take a single honours course in psychology and gain a wide understanding of the field, generally with the option to take optional courses in the second and third years. Joint honours degrees combine two relevant fields of study: for example, a degree combining psychology and business studies could be useful for someone who knew they wanted to go into occupational psychology. Careers suitable for psychology graduates are shown below.

## Some careers suitable for psychology graduates with no further study

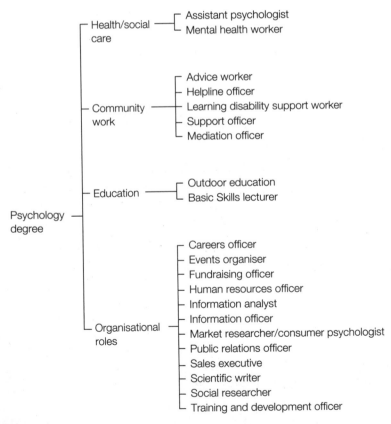

Psychology degree

Health/social care
- Assistant psychologist
- Mental health worker

Community work
- Advice worker
- Helpline officer
- Learning disability support worker
- Support officer
- Mediation officer

Education
- Outdoor education
- Basic Skills lecturer

Organisational roles
- Careers officer
- Events organiser
- Fundraising officer
- Human resources officer
- Information analyst
- Information officer
- Market researcher/consumer psychologist
- Public relations officer
- Sales executive
- Scientific writer
- Social researcher
- Training and development officer

Note, however, that a degree course can only give general information about any one specific area of work as a psychologist. This may be sufficient for many careers, but if you want to continue to a more specialised area of psychology, you will need to get a more advanced qualification, typically a master's or doctorate. To qualify with the British Psychological Society as a chartered psychologist you will need to have completed further study and also carried out work experience under the supervision of an accredited supervisor.

Examples of the various careers that involve some form of postgraduate study are shown in the figure below. Note that the distinctions between the various levels of postgraduate study are not always very clear. For example, a university lecturer may have a doctorate, a master's, or even some other form of professional qualification.

## Some careers suitable for psychology graduates after further study

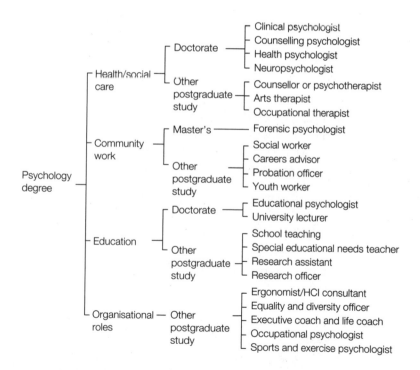

# ACCREDITATION

Throughout this book you will have seen many references to the British Psychological Society accreditation scheme. The following description is based directly on the process described on the BPS website (www.bps. org.uk), keeping the terminology used there.

Any psychology graduate can become a **Graduate Member** of the Society provided that they have one of the following:

- a pass in the Society's Qualifying Examination
- a Society-accredited honours degree in psychology
- a Society-accredited postgraduate qualification in psychology
- a Society-accredited conversion qualification.

However, to work as a **Chartered Psychologist** it is also necessary to:

- achieve the Graduate Basis for Registration
- undertake further Society-accredited training, and
- apply for entry onto the Register of Chartered Psychologists.

You will automatically have a **Graduate Basis for Registration** if you successfully follow a Society-accredited honours degree. The BPS website contains a list of all the accredited university courses. If your course is not accredited, or your degree is not in psychology, then you can gain GBR by:

- sitting the Society's qualifying examination, or
- taking a conversion course, which effectively converts your degree to the equivalent of an honours degree with psychology as the main subject.

**Society-accredited training** requirements vary with the particular field of psychology. However, they normally involve work experience under supervision by an experienced, accredited psychologist, and may also involve working on a research project. You can find the details in the relevant chapters of this book and on the BPS descriptions of the requirements for each specific field.

## Is accreditation essential?

There is no legal requirement to register as a chartered psychologist if you want to work as a psychologist. However, having accreditation confirms to employers and clients that you have been properly trained and qualified, and are answerable to an independent professional body.

If you want to assess the relevance of chartered status for your chosen field of psychology, try searching the various websites that show job vacancies. This will quickly give you a picture of the importance of accreditation in your chosen field.

## Conversion courses and qualifying examinations

Only certain degrees are accredited by the British Psychological Society. The most important factor is that they must cover the topics listed earlier in this chapter: biological, cognitive, developmental and social psychology, personality, the development of psychological concepts, and research methods.

Graduates of other degree courses may be able to join an accredited postgraduate course if they take a conversion course or are successful in a qualifying examination. This route is most likely to be followed by mature students who have carried out different types of learning during their career, or by students who have studied for a degree in which there was a significant input of psychological theory.

Full-time conversion courses typically last one or two years, the length depending largely on how many topics the students needs to cover. You can also complete distance learning conversion courses through the Open University and other university departments.

# THE CRIMINAL RECORDS BUREAU

Many psychologists work closely with children or with vulnerable adults. The Criminal Records Bureau is an agency of the Home Office that carries out checks on all those who work in this way. The aim is to stop employers in sensitive work of this type from employing anyone with a relevant criminal record.

When requested by a potential employer, the Bureau checks police records and, in relevant cases, information held by the Department of Health and the Department for Children, Schools and Families. There is a higher level of check (Enhanced Disclosure) available to anyone involved in regularly caring for, training, supervising or being in sole charge of children or vulnerable adults.

Do note, however, that the Rehabilitation of Offenders Act 1974 may apply. This is aimed at helping people who have been convicted of a criminal offence, received a sentence of not more than 2.5 years in prison and have not re-offended since that time. Offences of this type are not considered; though do note that there are certain exceptions, for example, linked to crimes of a sexual or violent nature.

# INTERNATIONAL STUDENTS

British universities attract large numbers of students from within the EU and from countries around the world. This applies to people wanting to study psychology just as much as it applies to any other field of study.

However, there may be difficulties for students wanting to continue their studies at postgraduate level with the aim of becoming chartered psychologists. These difficulties arise because of the element of work experience involved in gaining accreditation.

For example, if you apply for a clinical psychology training course you are applying for a job with the NHS. As a result, you will be classed as an employee. If you come from outside the European Economic Area (EEA) you would need a Tier 2 certificate of sponsorship (formerly a work permit); a student visa would not be sufficient. Such a work permit is unlikely to be granted, so universities are unlikely to accept applications from candidates from outside the EEA. Their main aim is to train clinical psychologists to work in the UK on a long-term basis.

If you come from within the EEA, the problem of the work permit does not arise. However, other issues can occur in, for example, forensic psychology. Courses in forensic psychology are based on the application of UK law; if you come from a country with a different system of laws, such as France, you will need to consider whether you will have the relevant understanding of the UK legal system. If you intend to return to France after your study, you will also need to consider whether your qualification will be recognised.

# WORK EXPERIENCE

You will have seen that work experience is an important factor at many stages of training to become a psychologist. Psychology is the study of people, their motivation, learning and emotions, and how they interact with the people and the world around them. For training and education in psychology to be effective, it must therefore be based on experience with people in the 'real world'. This is true for all study of psychology, but is particularly true if your work is going to be with people who are ill, psychologically damaged, suffer disability, may be a threat to themselves or others, and so on.

By gaining experience in the workplace you will also increase your own self-awareness, learning more about your particular skills, attributes and interests. You'll find out more about what particular types of work are like, and so get a better picture of how you want your career to progress. And you'll start to build a network of contacts, some of whom you may find will provide mutual support and guidance throughout your career.

## Pre-university experience

If you are at school or college, you can find useful experience by working on a voluntary scheme or a part-time job during weekends or holidays. Suitable examples might include working with youth groups or children's holiday programmes; coaching a local sport's team or working in a local arts' centre; or working in an old people's home.

Many universities will also consider a gap year between school and university as a useful experience, provided it involves relevant experiences. Using the year to work in, say, a school in the Third World will probably be considered more relevant than a year spent working in a fast-food outlet.

## Work experience while at university

Students can gain further useful experience by working part-time or on voluntary schemes while at university. Many universities will actively encourage students to find such work, and may include work placements as part of a four-year course.

Placements are particularly common in courses that focus on specific areas of psychology. For example, a course in sport and exercise psychology may well include placements in a local sports centre, health centres, a local NHS health promotion department, and with local sports clubs.

Some of the different types of work experience that may form part of a degree can be summarised as follows.

- **Work-based project:** a piece of work undertaken at an employer's premises, specifically linked to the course objectives, generally assessed by both workplace staff and your tutor.

- **Work placement:** a period of work experience (paid or unpaid), which forms part of your course of study. The arrangement with the employer may be made by the university or yourself.

- **Sandwich and industrial placements:** a fixed-term period of assessed, paid work that forms part of your degree. It often lasts for a full year. Sandwich placements often form part of a course that has been funded by a student's employer.

- **Internship:** a placement within a large organisation, usually during the summer vacation.

## Work experience as part of accreditation

The process of gaining accreditation and chartered status with the British Psychological Society always includes work experience related closely to the specific area of psychology.

For example, before students start training as educational psychologists they must generally demonstrate that they have at least a year's relevant experience of working with children in education, childcare, or in community work. On the doctorate programme the second and third years generally involve gaining practical experience by working for a local education authority as a trainee educational psychologist.

Similar involvement at work, gaining practical experience and applying the theory in practice, is an essential part of all training leading to chartered status. It is also an essential part of many other postgraduate programmes, such as the Certificate in Education needed by teachers and the various qualifications relating to counselling and psychotherapy.

# CONTINUING PERSONAL DEVELOPMENT

At whatever level you complete your study of psychology and enter the workplace, your training and learning should continue. Many organisations use the term 'continuing personal (or professional) development', better known as CPD.

The training may be through short courses, reading, attending conferences and networking. It may focus on specific aspects of psychology, for example a clinical psychologist may study more on new therapeutic techniques or a particular disorder, or a research assistant may study a particular statistical technique. It may be on using the equipment available within the organisation, such as the NHS's computer network or news software for statistical analysis. And finally, it could be in generic areas of study relating to work, such as time management, managing stress, or team-building.

If you want to move onwards to more senior positions you will also need to take specific courses in management skills, such as supervising trainees, staff appraisal, motivation, leadership and so on.

## Supervision

Supervision is one aspect of work as a psychologist that generally only applies to health-related organisations, particularly to those roles that involve therapeutic work with clients. The term is used in a particular way to describe regular meetings between the therapist and his or her supervisor. The aim of the meeting is to discuss and examine particular issues that have arisen during therapeutic work. Although there may be a certain degree to which the supervisor is 'checking up' on the therapist, the primary aim is to work together to provide the most effective work for the client. Seen in this way, supervision can be seen as another form of continuing personal development.

## ASSESSING YOUR OWN PROGRESS AND PLANS

As you read through this chapter on training, skills and qualifications, you may have asked yourself a 'chicken and egg' question. What must I think about first, the skills and qualifications I've got now or the skills and qualifications I will need to do a particular job?

It may be useful to develop your plans by thinking about that question in three stages.

1   Where am I now? What are my interests, skills, attributes and qualifications?

2   Where do I want to get to? What sort of work do I want to be doing in 5, 10 and 20 years' time?

3   How do I make the change? What work experience, study, skills and qualifications will I need?

If you are interested in one of the chartered psychologist careers described in Chapters 3 to 8, then you can link those three questions to the information given in those chapters. In particular, use the checklists at the end of each chapter to assess to what extent you could match the requirements of that job, and also enjoy the work.

If you want to consider one of the other careers suggested in Chapter 2, then you can find further information on the Prospects website (www.prospects.ac.uk). On the basis of those descriptions, and further research that you carry out using the web or careers guidance books and literature, you should be able to draw up similar checklists and assess whether you think a particular career is for you.

# Chapter Ten
# FINDING YOUR FIRST JOB

This chapter works through the process of applying for your first job, whether this is directly with an organisation or through a university that will provide a programme including work experience that will lead to further qualifications.

The process involves five steps.

**1**  Self-assessment, identifying your skills, attributes, personality, knowledge, qualifications and experience.

**2**  Comparing careers, trying to find the best match between your assessment and the various careers that are available.

**3**  Finding a suitable job, finding a specific vacancy or suitable course that will get you started on your career.

**4**  Demonstrating your competence, writing a tailored CV that will show a potential employer that you have the specific qualifications, skills and experience that they need.

**5**  Preparing for the interview, planning how you will respond to certain questions and ask your own questions.

# SELF-ASSESSMENT

The first step in finding a job is to carry out a self-assessment. This involves thinking about two primary questions.

**1** What sort of job do I want?

**2** Do I have the skills, attributes, personality, knowledge and experience that a potential employer will want?

Note the two ways of looking at yourself. Before applying for a job you need to check carefully that you really want to do the work. You also need to check that you are suitably qualified.

The following approach works through a self-assessment process in a systematic way, focusing on six key topics.

**1** Personal traits

**2** Personal values

**3** Economic needs

**4** Current skills

**5** Current knowledge and qualifications

**6** Future training needs.

## Personal traits

The aim here is to identify the words that best describe you. Some examples of traits could include being accurate, businesslike, cautious, decisive, easygoing and friendly.

Think first of all the words that describe you, writing them down relatively quickly as soon as they come into your mind. Take care that you record the traits you actually have, rather than the ones you might hope to have.

Then go through the list and identify the 10 that seem to be the most important. When you have 10, assess them and see if there are any important aspects of your personality that you have missed. If there are, you will have to decide whether to revise your list.

## Personal values

Where personal traits describe what you are like, personal values describe the principles that you think are important. Understanding your own values is crucial if you are to select a job that suits you. If having personal freedom is an important value, you will not want a job in which you work as a cog in an organisational machine from nine to five; if family relationships are not particularly important to you, you may be happy in a job that involves lots of travel.

The following are some examples of ways of working that would give someone a feeling of personal value: working creatively, being able to make decisions, being able to measure effectiveness and working independently.

Start by making a list of up to 10 values that you think are important in relation to your future work. Then briefly write a condition that would let you achieve that personal value. For example, if family relationships are important to you, you might set a condition that you would only work up to one weekend each month.

## Economic needs

Economic needs can be considered in three ways.

Firstly, how much do you need to earn to feel comfortable over the first year or two at work? You may also need to think about how you would feel if you were working as a trainee and so could expect to earn significantly more in two or three years' time?

Secondly, what would your needs be in the medium term? Remember that people's situations may change: people may get married, may have children, buy a house, inherit money from a wealthy relative, and so on. Thinking about the medium term may help you to decide between a high income now with little prospect of promotion, as compared with a lower current income but better long-term prospects.

Finally, getting to retirement age will seem a long way away for most students, but preparing for retirement is becoming increasingly important as more of us live longer. People who retire at 60 and live to 100 must expect to save enough during 40 years of work to support themselves for another 40 years. The pension arrangements for people working in the state sector generally offer significant advantages over those for workers in the private sector.

To assess your own economic needs, think in turn about each timescale. Note down any conditions about future pay and promotion that might make some work unsuitable.

## Current skills

Skills can be thought of under three broad headings.

Firstly, there are the core skills that you may have learned during your study of psychology. Examples of core skills could include being able to analyse numerical data or to summarise the findings of an academic study.

Secondly, there are specific skills that relate to your study. Examples here might include being able to carry out an assessment of somebody's reading age or IQ, identifying the early symptoms of Alzheimer's disease, or being able to analyse the interactions between the members of a team at work.

Finally, there are general skills that you may have learned in a range of situations. Perhaps you have learned to speak clearly while working with foreign language students; you may have developed a good memory while doing part-time work as a waiter; and your work at a call centre may have given you skills in dealing with anger.

Under the headings 'Core', 'General' and 'Specific', list all of the skills that you have. Then make another list showing, for each heading, the 10 skills that you feel are most important. Keep both lists: the 10 most important skills will help you to think about what jobs to apply for; the longer list will be useful when you look at the skills that a particular employer requires.

## Current knowledge and qualifications

It will be relatively easy to consider this topic if you have recently completed a degree course. It will be more difficult if your studies were some time ago, if your study involved a number of units from different courses or universities, or if some of your knowledge is based on practical experience rather than academic study.

The aim is to make a list of the areas of knowledge in which you feel competent. This will be based on the topic areas covered in your degree. However, you may be able to expand on the list if you have particular knowledge based on work experience or other study.

## Generic skills

During both your self-assessment and later, when writing your CV, you are likely to focus on the skills that relate directly to your chosen career or job. However, it's also useful to think about the generic skills that managers look for in graduates.

All successful graduates can be expected to show intellectual abilities, communication skills, knowledge of their subject and a positive attitude to learning. They are also likely to be self-motivated to be able to prioritise work and keep to deadlines.

On the other hand, potential employers will not be able to assume that all graduates have the following attributes.

- **Flexibility:** how can you show an employer that you will be able to adjust to changing requirements at work?

- **Self-assurance:** does your CV show a suitable level of self-confidence, without appearing arrogant?

- **Interpersonal skills:** this is an important requirement for many jobs as a psychologist. How can you use the work experience section of your CV to show that you have successfully related to a range of people at work?

- **Teamwork:** this is also an important requirement for many jobs as a psychologist. Again, your success as a team-worker can be shown by describing your work experience, and perhaps some of your out-of-work activities.

## Future training needs

As you begin to think about particular jobs, you are likely to find that they require certain skills that you lack. Don't panic at this stage: employers rarely find a candidate who fills absolutely all of the requirements on their job description.

However, it is important to identify these skills gaps, so that you can plan how you might fill them in the future. You need to check that your future employer will enable you to take further training so that you can carry out all of your work effectively. Employers will also be impressed at an interview if you are able to show awareness of particular skills gaps and have planned how they could be filled.

It may also be that you can fill certain skills gaps quite quickly. For example, many graduate jobs require skills in using word processing and spreadsheet packages, and some require skills in using desktop publishing or project management programs. All of those skills could be gained quickly by taking computer courses before you graduate, or by going to evening classes in a local college before you go for a job interview.

## Overview of your self-assessment

Having thought about, and made notes on, the six topics, you should be better able to think about the two primary questions.

- What sort of job do I want?

- Do I have the skills, attributes, personality, knowledge and experience that a potential employer will want?

Do note that it is often useful to discuss your assessment with someone, perhaps a careers advisor, a family member or a colleague. Explaining your ideas to another person often clarifies your thoughts; you may realise that you are making exaggerated claims in some areas, and the other person may be able to suggest some skills or attributes that you have missed.

## Using case studies

This book contains case studies for each of the careers described in Chapters 3 to 8. You can find further examples of case studies on the various careers websites, such as www.bps.co.uk and www.prospects. ac.uk.

Studying case studies of people who work in particular fields will often give you a 'feel' for what each job involves. After completing your self-assessment, and provisionally deciding on a particular career, it will be useful to study the case studies. Can you see yourself in that role?

# COMPARING CAREERS

Having assessed yourself, and identified what you are looking for in a career, you are now ready to compare different careers.

Using the approach used in Chapters 3 to 8, you should generally consider each of the following headings in turn. Some key questions have been included in the list, but you are likely to have further specific questions of your own.

| | |
|---|---|
| **A typical case load** | Who are the clients? |
| | What tasks (e.g. assessment, therapy, research, health promotion) are involved? |
| | Would I work with individuals, independently, with a team, or a mixture of all three? |
| **The work setting** | Who are the employers: the NHS, local authorities or large companies? |
| | What are the hours of work, and does it involve weekend or evening work? |
| | Is the work based in large cities and town, or throughout the UK? |
| | How much travel is involved? What are the opportunities for part-time working, or consultancy? |
| **Qualifications required** | Does this post require a degree, master's or doctorate? |
| | What work experience is required? |
| | Can I get further work experience while completing a higher qualification? |
| **Case studies** | After reading the case study in this book, and others on careers websites, can I see myself in this role? |

*(Continued)*

*(Continued)*

| | |
|---|---|
| **The practicalities** | How stressful is the work? |
| | How much support, training and development are available? |
| **Career progression** | What are the levels of pay? |
| | What are the chances of promotion? |
| **Skills and attributes** | Do I have the skills needed? |
| | Do I have the relevant attributes? |
| **Highs and lows** | What are the highs and lows? |
| | To what extent would the highs motivate me and give me job satisfaction? |
| | How would I be affected by the lows, and how would I deal with them? |
| | Overall, how would I feel when doing this job? |

# FINDING A SUITABLE JOB

On the basis of your self-assessment and your survey of the various careers, you should now be ready to start looking for a particular job. For many graduates, this will involve applying directly to a potential employer; for those hoping to work towards chartered status or some other further qualification, it may involve applying to a university for a postgraduate programme.

You can find many jobs for psychologists in newspaper recruitment pages, such as in the *Guardian* (http://jobs.guardian.co.uk), or on the websites of large employers, such as www.jobs.nhs.uk.

There may also be posts for new graduates on the www.prospects.ac.uk website and members of the British Psychological Society can find information on psychologist appointments on http://www.psychapp.co.uk.

## Job titles

As you search the various websites, do note that similar jobs with different organisations may appear under different job titles. In addition, the same job title may be used to describe quite different work in different organisations.

So, for example, very similar work may be carried out by a training officer in one organisation and by a learning and development officer in another. On the other hand, the title 'public relations officer' may be used for someone working in a local authority or a commercial company, but the work they would do could be quite different.

### Finding out more

Having identified a relatively short list of possible jobs, you need to try to find out as much as you can about the work, the employers, the area, and so on.

You can often find information of this type in a public or university library, and a great deal can also be found by searching on the web. For example, entering the terms 'working in the NHS' will bring up a great deal of recruitment information from, for example, NHS trusts; but it will also link to newspaper articles about NHS work, and sites where people comment on their work experiences.

A great deal of detailed information about local areas is available on the web, for example on the Up My Street website (www.upmystreet.com).

# DEMONSTRATING YOUR COMPETENCE

If you are to get the job that you have chosen, then you are going to need to demonstrate to an employer, or a university department, that you have the skills, knowledge and attributes that will be needed.

Assuming that you have identified a particular job and have used all the various ways of collecting information about the job, the employer, the area, and so on, you are now ready to write a tailored CV (*curriculum vitae*, meaning 'course of life').

### Writing a tailored CV

Note the key word 'tailored' applied to a CV. It is relatively easy to write a list of the qualifications, skills and experience that you have. Unfortunately, writing an effective CV is a more complex task: you have to market yourself, showing that the qualifications, skills and experience that you have exactly match those required by the potential employer.

Your CV should include:

- your contact details (name, address, email address, land and mobile phone numbers)

- a brief overview of why you think you are suitable for the particular post

- your education and qualifications, showing the degree subject, class (or predicted class), the modules studied, A-levels (with dates and grades) and a summary of your GCSEs/O-levels or CSEs

- a description of your skills, focusing on the core, specific and general ones that are relevant to this particular job

- a summary of your work experience, again focusing on the areas that are relevant for the particular job

- your referees (provided you have asked their permission first) or an offer to provide referees' names and contact details on request.

You can find detailed guidance on writing a CV in your university's (or school's) career's library, on university websites, or by searching elsewhere on the web. You can also use the presentation tools available in many word processing packages.

## Gaps in your CV

As you write your CV you may find that there are topics that you don't want to highlight. Perhaps you had to retake some A-levels, had to repeat a year at university, had a job that only lasted a few weeks, or may have a criminal record.

The key point is that you must complete your CV honestly. Any inaccuracies on a CV can give an employer grounds to dismiss you immediately for 'gross misconduct'.

However, it would probably be acceptable not to mention a retake of A-levels, that you repeated a year at university, or similar examples. The CV is meant to be a summary of your achievements rather than a detailed analysis of your life. On the other hand, be prepared for a potential employer to ask why, for example, your degree course took an extra year.

The question of a criminal record is more complex. After a certain time period (which varies depending on the particular offence) you do not need to mention a criminal record to potential employers, provided that the punishment was less than 2.5 years in prison and you have not re-offended. For details of this, refer to information on the Rehabilitation of Offenders Act 1974. However, there are certain exceptions, for example linked to crimes of a sexual or violent nature.

# THE INTERVIEW

Employers filter all applications, so most people invited for interview will have the qualifications and skills needed to do the job. In most cases, interviewers will want to discuss some details relating to your CV, talk about your career aims and assess how well you will fit into the organisation and your work team. They also want to give you a chance to find out more about the organisation; they do not want to employ someone who then leaves quickly because the work was not what they expected.

## Some possible questions

Questions will typically fall into three groups: relating to you, your studies and qualifications, and your knowledge of the employer.

Examples of questions about yourself could include asking you to describe yourself, your motivation, or your strengths and weaknesses. They may also relate to practical questions, such as whether you will need to travel considerable distances to the workplace, your long-term goals or the work environment in which you feel most comfortable.

Questions about your studies could be about why you chose your university, why you chose psychology, and what aspects of your studies you liked most and least. Interviewers may also ask you to talk about how you think your study will prepare you for the work you have chosen, and whether your academic achievements accurately indicate your ability and potential at work. Questions about your work experience will typically ask you to describe what they have taught you and how you might apply the experiences to your future work.

Finally, the interviewers will ask you questions about what you know about the organisation. These will generally have two aims: first, to assess whether you have done your research and found out about the organisation; second, to confirm that you have thought about how well you would fit into their organisation and its culture.

## Planning your own questions

Towards the end of an interview, candidates are generally asked if they have their own questions. This serves two purposes. First, the interviewers can use it to assess whether you have researched the organisation. They will quickly notice if you ask about something that is answered on the homepage of the company website.

More importantly, by asking any final questions you can fill in any gaps in your understanding of the job or the organisation. Interviews are not only about whether you will be accepted for the post; they are also about a chance to find out whether you want the particular job.

Some possible questions could focus on the specific responsibilities, opportunities and challenges of the job; and on possible career paths and opportunities for training and development. You could ask about what a typical day in this post might involve. Or you could ask more general questions about the future prospects for the organisation.

## The end of the interview

Interviewers will generally follow a strict timetable, so will show clearly that they are bringing the interview to an end. Be careful not to prolong the discussion, but do make sure that you know what is going to happen next. How will you find out if you have been successful? If unsuccessful, can you get feedback?

## Reasons why people fail at interviews

Some of the most common reasons that managers give for candidates failing at interviews can be summarised as follows.

- **Appearance.** Interviews are formal situations, so interviewers generally expect you to dress suitably.

- **Lack of research.** Prepare for the interview by finding out as much as you can about the organisation and the role.

- **Lack of preparation.** Anticipate the questions that the interviewer might ask. In particular, be ready to show how your skills and experience match the requirements of the job.

- **Failing the basics.** Turn up on time. If you are unavoidably late, give as much notice as possible and be ready to explain why you are late.

- **Lack of enthusiasm, or excessive enthusiasm.** You need to show that you are enthusiastic about the work, but you also need to show that you are using the interview as your final check on whether the job suits you.

- **Negativity.** Never make critical comments about your current work, since interviewers will wonder what you might think about your new job. You may be able to sound more positive by talking about wanting to have new challenges or work as a member of a team.

- **Failing to listen.** Listen carefully to what the interviewers tell you about the organisation, and try to show how your skills, experience and personality will fit with their requirements.

- **Lack of supporting evidence.** Make sure that you give evidence and stories to show that you have the relevant skills, attributes and experience.

- **Lying, or exaggerating.** If you are caught lying, that will be the end of the interview. Describe your achievements accurately, remembering that interviewers will usually know if you are exaggerating.

## Getting feedback

Interviews are used to select the most suitable candidates from a shortlist, all of whom satisfy the main criteria. That means that many, very suitable candidates will be rejected.

If you are rejected, you can often get useful information by asking for feedback. This may give you some consolation (for example, if the interviewer comments, 'You were one of the final three that we considered'). More important, it will give you factual information that you may be able to use in future applications (for example, if you were told, 'The successful candidate had more experience in hospital work', you might need to explain in future interviews that the clinic in which you worked was part of a hospital).

Finally, don't forget the benefits of networking. It is almost certain that someone within your friends, colleagues or relations will either work, or know someone who works, for the NHS, for another large employer, or knows about a particular region of the country.

# NETWORKING

You saw earlier the benefits of using a network of friends, colleagues and other contacts to collect information about organisations; regions, cities and towns, job vacancies, courses and work experience opportunities. You can also build your network in organisations where you have had an interview. You may not have been selected this time, but a more suitable opportunity may come up in the future.

The development of the Internet has also enormously expanded the opportunity for networking, for example through sites that link people from particular schools, colleges or universities. There are also networks of people working in particular careers.

However, networking must be carried out ethically. You are sharing information, not asking for a back-door entry to a new post. Remember also that any contact you make with a potential employer will be judged just as carefully as your CV or your interview.

# Chapter Eleven
# CAREER PROGRESSION

In the preceding chapters the focus has primarily been on how you build on a degree in psychology and start on a career.

For many people, that career will provide a stable pathway throughout a lifetime at work. They may be a trainee at 25, a chartered psychologist at 30, a senior psychologist at 45 and retire as a head of a department at 60.

For others, a career may involve a number of sideways steps as they move into areas that interest them. For example, a person may work towards the qualifications for chartered status as a mature student, may later move into academic work at a university, and gradually move towards consultancy work.

This chapter highlights some of the factors that relate to career choices and changes at different stages of life. Those factors can be summarised as follows.

- **Salary.** What are the financial benefits and costs of staying in a single career, or moving into different fields?

- **Accreditation.** How important is accreditation? What are the benefits and costs for the individual?

- **Changing specialisms.** What are the key points to think about before deciding to change to a different field or specialism in mid-career? How do you get started in consultancy?

- **Predicting future changes.** To what extent is it possible to predict what will happen in your current career?

# SALARY

You will have seen various salaries given in the different chapters covering specific careers. Note that these are typical 2009 figures and do not include additional payments such as a London weighting. In other words, they are useful when comparing typical salary levels, but you should make sure that you refer to current job advertisements for more detailed information.

Remember that salary levels are not the only financial factor to consider. For example, some trainee jobs in the NHS may include housing, some public sector workers in London may be eligible for help with their housing or mortgage payments, you may find a job with a company car, work in certain industries may attract share or other bonuses, and so on.

Remember also the question of pension contributions. There are often tax benefits to both yourself and your company from pension payments being taken directly from your pay, and from the company contributing a further sum to your pension fund.

Finally, consider the costs that you may have as a result of having a particular job. The further away your place of work is from home, the more you will have to pay in travel costs; and the more you may have to pay in childcare if you have a family.

## Pay scales

Depending on your chosen career, you may also find it useful to refer to national pay scales, such as the NHS pay rates (see www.nhscareers. nhs.uk).

When you study pay scales, you will notice that they gradually rise so that more experienced employees get paid more than newcomers to the post. If you have above the minimum qualifications and experience for a post, you may start a few steps up the pay scale. The system of gradually increasing pay acts as an incentive to stay in a post for a certain time.

## Salaries over three timescales

As you saw in Chapter 10, you need to consider salaries over three timescales. Firstly, how much do you need to earn to feel comfortable over the first year or two at work? Secondly, what would your needs be in the medium term? Finally, what are the arrangements for pensions? If you expect to be retired for up to 40 years after working for 40 years, you will need to consider this issue from when you start work.

In relation to career progression, the second two questions are of greatest importance. If you ignore your medium-term needs, you may find that you experience problems if you, for example, want to buy a house, get married, have children, or even want to enjoy expensive holidays. For many this question is about balancing job satisfaction against future income: if you happily go into a low-paid job after your university study, can you be sure that you will not regret your decision at a later stage? For others the question relates to balancing low income while training against the potential of high earnings later.

In relation to pension provision, the Association of Consulting Actuaries advises 25-year-olds to save 15% of their annual salary every year to guarantee a 'comfortable retirement'. Working for the state (for example in the NHS, education, or for local authorities), or for most large organisations, some pension contributions will automatically be deducted from your salary, but this may not be so when working for smaller organisations.

# ACCREDITATION

## The benefits of accreditation

Psychologists working in a number of fields may gain accreditation from professional bodies. You will have seen many references in this book to the British Psychological Society (BPS), which accredits, for example, forensic, clinical and educational psychologists. In the health field, psychotherapists may be accredited through the United Kingdom

Council for Psychotherapy (UKCP) or the British Association for Counselling and Psychotherapy (BACP). There are many other industry-specific organisations, such as the Chartered Institute of Marketing (CIM) and the Chartered Institute of Personnel and Development (CIPD).

The benefits of accreditation can be described under three headings.

■ **Professional standards.** Membership of a professional organisation gives employers and clients some confidence that you have the relevant skills, qualification and experience to carry out your role successfully. Research findings and other papers produced by the professional body pass on relevant information about the effectiveness of particular ways of working. Many professional bodies produce a journal of papers reporting members' research or opinions.

■ **Professional community.** The professional body acts as a network, giving information and allowing members to meet and discuss their practice. Many professional bodies produce training and educational materials, and accredit courses that lead to professional qualifications.

■ **Pay and conditions.** Many of the various professional bodies are involved in pay agreements and give guidance on the pay and conditions that should apply to their members. Many employers then specify that employees in particular roles must be accredited by a suitable professional body.

## The costs of accreditation

There are, however, certain costs of accreditation for individuals. The process of becoming accredited can take many years (for example, accreditation as a clinical psychologist generally takes three years of postgraduate study and work experience). During this three-year period you may be earning at rates significantly lower than you could get in other careers.

There is also the financial cost of paying membership fees each year to the professional body. For example, annual membership fees (2009) are £109 for the BPS and £121 for the CIPD per year. You may also need to consider the costs of attending conferences and meetings.

# CHANGING SPECIALISMS

The descriptions of particular careers in this book have inevitably focused on those who follow a gradual, systematic career progression. This typically involves starting with a psychology degree, moving on to further qualifications and work experience, starting work at the entrant levels in the profession, and then following a gradual progression to senior roles.

In practice, many people follow more complex career paths. The clinical psychologist may develop an interest in psychotherapy and train to become a counselling psychologist. A graduate nurse may use his or her degree and further training in psychology to move out of nursing into work as a mental health policy officer. A special needs teacher may gradually gain suitable qualifications and experience that will enable him or her to get a post as a lecturer in a university education department.

If you think you may want to change specialisms now, or in the future, you need to follow a process involving many of the tasks outlined in Chapter 10.

- Self-assessment, identifying your skills, attributes, personality, knowledge, qualifications and experience.

- Considering the new career, assessing whether there is a good match between your assessment and the career you are considering.

- Finding a suitable job, finding a specific vacancy or suitable course that will get you started on your new career.

- Checking that you could demonstrate your competence, writing a tailored CV that would show a potential employer that you have the specific qualifications, skills and experience that they need.

## Assessing your current job

When thinking about your career now and in the future, you also need to consider your working conditions and job satisfaction. As some examples, try thinking about the following questions.

- Imagine working in the same job in five or ten years' time. What is your first reaction?

- Do you feel that your job is secure?

- Do you feel satisfied if you have completed a particular task?

- Do you feel that your efforts are recognised and appreciated?

- Do you have good relations with your work colleagues?

- If you continue in your current job until you retire, with promotion if relevant, will you look back and feel satisfied?

If you are dissatisfied, then it will be useful to investigate other workplaces or careers to see whether your needs would be better satisfied in another career or another workplace. However, do take care to assess your options carefully: there is always a risk of seeing the benefits of new possibilities without noticing the disadvantages that will always be present. As always, it is essential to use your networks to get an accurate picture.

## Consultancy and freelance work

If you are in mid-career and feel that you want new experiences, an alternative to completely changing career is to move into consultancy or freelance work. You may be able to combine this with working part-time, an approach that gives you some security while developing your new career.

Consultancy does involve a significant risk that the level of work will be low, especially when you first start. If you aim to continue working in the same geographical area, it may be that you can build your networks before leaving your permanent post and so start your new venture with a number of potentially useful contacts. Do be aware, however, of the ethical questions involved. It would, for example, be highly unethical for an NHS psychotherapist setting up a private practice to try to contact potential clients from the NHS waiting list. There are also more complex issues around using NHS facilities for private consultations or looking for referrals from an NHS GP.

As with all career moves, the key is to consider certain essential questions before deciding to make any change. Many of these will be the same as you should ask when making any career move. However, there are some specific ones relating to consultancy work; for example, whether you really want to work independently, whether there is likely to be a large enough pool of clients, whether you feel confident 'selling' your services, how you will insure yourself or maintain your professional body membership, and so on.

# PREDICTING FUTURE CHANGES

Certain types of psychologist will always be required in relatively predictable numbers. For example, the school population is relatively steady, and the proportion of children needing special help is also relatively stable; it therefore seems likely that the requirement for educational psychologists will remain relatively constant. You might even predict a gradual rise in the requirement as people become more aware of problems like autism and dyslexia.

On the other hand, the role of health psychologist is relatively new. It has been an increasingly popular field of study at university and increasing numbers of health psychologists have been recruited in hospitals and rehabilitation centres. However, it is difficult to predict at what rate the requirement for health psychologists will grow over future years. One key issue is whether health promotion will increasingly be based on central government programmes, or whether it will be developed locally by health psychologists.

In private organisations there is the further issue of the economic climate. During an economic downturn it may be that organisations will cut the number of employees, perhaps starting with those not involved directly in production or contact with customers. In other words, it may be that psychologists and those in allied careers will be among the first people to lose their jobs.

One useful way of assessing future changes is to use your professional body and your network of friends, colleagues and contacts. All of you have a mutual interest in being kept up to date with trends in your field, and with economic and organisational changes that may affect you in the future.

# Chapter Twelve
# FINDING OUT MORE

Throughout this book you will have seen suggestions about where you can find further information. This chapter gives details of the various organisations, and some others that you may want to refer to if you have an interest in a particular type of work using psychological skills and qualifications.

## INFORMATION FOR ALL PSYCHOLOGISTS

For information on the wide range of careers available to psychologists, the qualifications needed for each one, and for detailed information on the accreditation process, you need to refer to the British Psychological Society (BPS).

**The British Psychological Society (BPS)**
St Andrews House, 48 Princess Road East
Leicester LE1 7DR
0116 254 9568
www.bps.org.uk

## INFORMATION ON SPECIFIC FIELDS OF PSYCHOLOGY

Next, there are many organisations that provide specific information about careers for psychologists working in particular fields. Note that in some cases you can find further information in Chapters 3 to 8 of this book.

**Association of Business Psychologists (ABP)**
211/212 Piccadilly
London W1J 9HG
020 7917 1733
www.theabp.org.uk

**Association of Educational Psychologists (AEP)**
4 The Riverside Centre
Frankland Lane
Durham DH1 5TA
0191 384 5912
www.aep.org.uk

**British Association for Counselling and Psychotherapy (BACP)**
BACP House
15 St John's Business Park
Lutterworth LE17 4HB
01455 883300
www.bacp.co.uk

**British Association for Sport and Exercise Sciences (BASES)**
Leeds Metropolitan University
Carnegie Faculty of Sport and Education
Fairfax Hall, Headingley Campus
Beckett Park
Leeds LS6 3QS
0113 812 6162
www.bases.org.uk

**The Health Professions Council (HPC)**
Park House
184 Kennington Park Road
London SE11 4BU
020 7582 0866
www.hpc-uk.org

**HM Prison Service**
www.hmprisonservice.gov.uk

**Improvement and Development Agency (I&DeA)**
Layden House
76–86 Turnmill Street
London EC1M 5LG
020 7296 6680
www.idea.gov.uk

**United Kingdom Council for Psychotherapy (UKCP)**
2nd Floor, Edward House
2 Wakley Street
London EC1V 7LT
020 7014 9955
www.psychotherapy.org.uk

# CAREERS INFORMATION AND JOB VACANCIES

Certain organisations provide web-based information on careers and list job vacancies. Some of these cater for the whole of the job market; others focus on specific types of work. Some that are particular relevant for psychologists are shown below. Note that some organisations are purely web-based and should not be contacted by post or telephone.

**Prospects, a guide to graduate careers**
Graduate Prospects
Booth Street East
Manchester M13 9EP
0161 277 5200
www.prospects.ac.uk

**British Psychological Society: appointments**
BPS Communications
St Andrews House
48 Princess Road East
Leicester LE1 7DR
0116 254 9568
www.psychapp.co.uk

**NHS Careers**
PO Box 2311
Bristol BS2 2ZX
0845 606 0655
www.nhscareers.nhs.uk
www.stepintothenhs.nhs.uk

**Improvement and Development Agency (I&DeA)**
Layden House
76–86 Turnmill Street
London EC1M 5LG
020 7296 6680
www.lgcareers.com
www.lgjobs.com

Note that all telephone numbers show the codes to be used in the UK. To telephone an organisation from outside the UK, replace the initial 0 with 44. For example, to contact the UK number 020 7296 6680 from outside the UK, ring 44 20 7296 6680.

# FURTHER READING

- The British Psychological Society produce *The Psychologist*, a journal of relevance to those working in many areas of psychology.

- A range of NHS careers leaflets can be downloaded or ordered from the NHS careers website, www.nhscareers.nhs.uk/downloads.shtml

- *So You Want to be a Psychologist?* provides a summary of many careers in psychology and the qualifications necessary for each one. It is available most easily if you search for the title on the BPS website (www.bps.org.uk).

- A number of journals are produced by the various professional bodies, such as the CIPD's *People Management* for those working in personnel and development, or *Educational Psychology in Practice*.